BUSINESS POWER AND PUBLIC POLICY

Alfred C. Neal

PRAEGER

PRAEGER SPECIAL STUDIES • PRAEGER SCIENTIFIC

Library of Congress Cataloging in Publication Data

Neal, Alfred Clarence.
  Business power and public policy.

  1. Committee for Economic Development.
2. United States—Economic policy—1971-
3. Industry and state—United States. 4. Industry
—Social aspects—United States. I. Title.
HC106.7.N43   338.973   81-7348
ISBN 0-03-060268-8 (pb)   AACR2
ISBN 0-03-059586-X (hb)

338.973
N338b

Published in 1981 by Praeger Publishers
CBS Educational and Professional Publishing
a Division of CBS Inc.
521 Fifth Avenue, New York, New York 10175 U.S.A.

© 1981 by Praeger Publishers   82-8960

123456789   145   987654321

Printed in the United States of America

FOREWORD

Philip M. Klutznick

As I write these words, my service as secretary of commerce in the Carter administration draws to a close. The national elections that many think turned on the condition of the economy are over. Like all political campaigns the air was full of exaggerations about the desperate state to which we have fallen. At the close serious consideration was given by members of the new administration to declaring an economic emergency reminiscent of FDR's first 100 days. A bit of window dressing was suggested in the use of the phrase "Economic Dunkirk." Fortunately, more mature thoughts emerged. You cannot rescue an economy with boats — what is needed is a factual base and ideas, not pap and propaganda. Comparing our present economic predicament with FDR's 100 days may give emotional relief, but it offers very little substantive treatment to the underlying ills that beset the economy of the 1980s.

It is important to know something of the 1930s, the Great Depression, the hesitant recovery, and the evolution to a peerless economic summit by the United States following World War II. I am grateful to my dear friend Alfred C. Neal for *Business Power and Public Policy*. I only wish it had been available some months earlier. Those who are grappling with our economic ills should privilege themselves to a careful reading of the experiences and ideas that come from the mind and pen of the former president of the Committee for Economic Development (CED). Business leadership and the community at large might develop a more sane approach to our present predicament by a thorough reading of this work.

Himself a highly qualified economist and teacher, Neal had the benefit of more than 20 years of leadership of the CED during which he was at the center of academic-business studies and thought, as well as government relationships, involving a wide variety of key economic-political-social issues. It was during his stewardship that many of the most significant ideas and recommendations of the CED were conceived and published.

The differences in perception and understanding of the key issues of our times are dictated in large measure by the teachers and associates with whom one works and studies. Over a period of 20 years of activity as a trustee, as chairman of Research and Policy, and as vice-chairman of the Board of Trustees of the CED, I have stood witness to the development of greater comprehension and appreciation by key business leaders and academicians as they struggled with some of the most pressing economic and national challenges of our day. I believe myself a personal beneficiary of that process that stretches the mind.

The author accords me the honor of citing at length excerpts from an address I delivered as chairman of Research and Policy on January 9, 1975, when the economy was once again in trouble. As I read these quotes, I was pleased that I had given this speech. I remain grateful for its aftereffects. But it is only fair to give credit where credit is due. It was the benefits of my experiences in the CED plus the valuable and exceptionally talented staff advice that molded the thoughts I expressed.

One can only expect Neal's discussions of significant but limited aspects of his vast background to serve as a guide to more sober and meaningful thought on the urgent economic challenges of the hour. As I read through the record of some familiar recent economic history, I began to understand once more how helpful it is to look backward as a prelude to looking forward. The author will excite and even disturb some by his forthright and resourceful observations. Some trite views widely held melt under citation of fact and reality.

As we approached the windup of World War II, some farsighted business leaders envisioned turbulent economic problems ahead. Out of their wisdom there emerged the CED. Men such as Jesse Jones, Paul Hoffman, William Benton, Ralph Flanders, Marion Folsom, David Zellerbach, Donald David, and others brought together top U.S. business leaders and able academicians. Out of their vision came what has since been identified as the CED process. The author describes this process in detail and in its several varied forms in Chapter 1. Reading and studying this technique are keys to understanding the CED. The process served not only to develop thought and ideas and, normally, a substantial consensus, but, perhaps more important, it continued to excite men and women of affairs and academicians to participate. Successful volunteerism depends on the urge to be involved. In this regard, the CED organizational structure achieved a high level of acceptance.

It is out of this process of thinking together that basic portions of this book arose. If there were only the time and patience in the day-to-day life of our free nation to afford people adequate access to facts and ideas as well as the opportunity to reason together, how different our nation would be. Stretching our minds to reach for agreement in place of exercising our voices to magnify dissent is the desperate need of our society. We live these days with continuous exposure to conclusions and views without time to analyze and think about those conclusions and views. The private sector's adversarial attitude toward government and vice versa could be turned around so that both may sink their energies into working toward more solutions to deep-rooted economic and social problems. A democratic society needs a CED-type process to avoid the inevitable mistakes arising from instantaneously available conflicting views and ideas.

Chapter 2, "National Economic Planning — Business and Government Roles," presents fresh views on vital topics. The author is at his best in delineating the roles of government. There has been and there is planning in process even now in the public sector. It would be tragic if this were not so. Neal is clear in his descriptions of this activity. It was Heine, I believe, who said, "We learn from history that we learn nothing from history." Each generation tends to "know not Joseph." New U.S. leadership arises in each generation. Whether they are governmental, business, labor, or social leaders, they tend to forget or know not of the recent past. As the last days of World War II brought mournful predictions of forthcoming widespread unemployment as millions demobilized, the nation was little prepared to meet the hunger for things that accumulated after 16 years of spotty recovery from the Great Depression followed by years of war. The author reminds us that we still had 16 percent unemployed as World War II began. Some official and unofficial estimates of postwar unemployment reaching 10 million were circulating.

The destruction of the vast industrial capacity of Western Europe and Japan and the growing demands of a shrinking world provided both government and industry with new economic challenges. Both government and business undertook the task of promoting high employment and stabilizing the economy. Laissez-faire had been buried by the depression. Now the task began in earnest of how to use government intervention and preserve a free economy. The CED's role on this front has never ceased to this day. The history of the immediate postwar period is good background for those charged with present-day economic responsibilities.

The reality of a new distribution of economic power following World War II has never been totally appreciated or understood. A United States with nearly one-half of the world's gross national product — and even now with about one-fourth of a much larger pie — rose to new heights of political and economic statesmanship. It was an institution like the CED that helped break new ground in seeking prosperity, full employment, and an improvement in the quality of life for Americans — and with understanding and compassion for the recovering and developing world.

But even as the United States emerged as the giant of industrial and economic development, so were there many concomitant internal changes in production and capitalization, as well as in economic and legal theory. The book illustrates in several of the chapters a theory that we accept that hardly conforms to practices that prevail. Chapters 4 through 8 — "The Erosion of Business Capital," "The Social Responsibilities of Large Companies," "Ideological Conflict over the Power of Unions," "Corporate Size and Cost-Price Behavior," and "Roles of the Large Company in the Real American Economy" — are exciting, and many may find them revolutionary in thought. But they tell it as it is. The scabs are torn away to disclose reality.

Over a long generation after the end of World War II, Neal's book reveals a dizzying progression of old problems and new ones that business statesmen and scholars tried to study and understand. The concept of a federal budget based on the principle of stabilizing the economy did not prove automatic in implementation. Emergency fiscal and monetary policies and voluntary and even mandatory wage and price policies needed analyses and understanding.

In a fast-moving universe the interrelations between domestic objectives and worldwide economic developments had to become more important. Even the friends whose economic recovery we aided and the developing nations whose economic ambitions we abetted became not only our customers but our competitors as well. The impact on the U.S. share of the world's business helped create and aggravate growing domestic economic difficulties.

Declining rates of productivity growth, succeeding periods of inflation and deflation, declining savings, and capital investment all provided key topics for business and academic investigation and study. The CED continued to expand its horizons. At the same time, in its own unique business fashion it addressed the role and function of large companies in the arena of social action. The concept of socially responsible behavior provided one of the most stimulating chapters of CED history. Not far removed from this generic idea was the statesmanlike treatment of "union power" and such emerging problems as corporate size and its impact on cost-price behavior.

For the first time this book relies on records of intimate discussions among business leaders and academicians on a whole variety of topics. It is a measure of the confidence in Neal by the leaders of the organization he served so well and so long that they voted him full access to this valued treasury, with a reservation against attribution. We have here a sensitive use by a responsible and knowledgeable person of a wealth of material covering one of the most volatile and exciting economic periods in U.S. history.

In these days when a new set of economic challenges faces us, it might profit government, business, and labor leaders to rely on the proved merit of the CED approach. It relied on the study and conclusions reached by persons of differing views to make workable solutions rather than short-term slogans and quick fixes. If this experience proves anything, it establishes the reality that in a free society the economy is subject to many influences. Like a living person it gets its periods of illness as well as its times of health. When it develops a cold, it is important to diagnose it as a cold and not as pneumonia. When we get reckless and let our aspirations exceed our capacities, the source of our economic backache must not provide a dosage that treats cancer.

As Neal suggests, we not only need thoughtful processes of diagnosis, but we also need to invite the strengths of government and the private sector to provide the remedies. When the CED helped preside over the nonacceptance of laissez-faire as the solution to our economic needs, it was inevitable that we began a period of realization that the public and private sectors must abandon hostility against one another. It is the demand of the hour that we maintain the tension of reasonable differences while we seek to attain the maximum of cooperation between government, business, and labor. Therein is the logical consequence of the lessons expressed and unexpressed in this timely book.

The proposal to use government/private sector collaboration with a base that Neal identifies as 600+ is intriguing. But in some respects, it is almost too idealistic. In my limited experiences in the U. S. Department of Commerce, we undertook a more modest collaboration than the 600+. It involved sectoral groups such as aerospace, the aluminum industry, and fisheries. We undertook a tripartite approach (government, business, and labor) in the steel and automobile industries. In a sense, we reduced Neal's generic concept of 600+ to workable proportions. This collaborative approach, whether on a broader base or more widespread, is an inescapable next step in our nation's economic development.

One final plug for my old friend and teacher, Al Neal. He has put into one volume a full platter of stimulating challenges. He has shown appropriate respect for economists while simultaneously pointing out some conspicuous failures. I would hope that the Reagan administration would grasp the challenges posed in this work. Perhaps a commission of representative and forward-looking leaders of business, labor, and academicians could use the book as a base and produce a workable program that would get at the sources of our present economic predicament. On several occasions since World War II we have tried some, or a combination of, old-time remedies that worked in a different day and a different world.

The U.S. economy in its domestic aspects and in its competitive relationship to the world is stronger and more vigorous than some of its politically motivated detractors tend to claim. Nevertheless, there are some patent and deep-seated questions that need courageous responses. Neal has rendered a unique service in posing many of these questions and has either given or implied some answers. It is time that government, industry, labor, and society face up to the real problems we have together created — out of this can come solutions instead of palliatives.

PREFACE

This book grew out of a realization that society would be richer if the escape of knowledge as a result of the neglect and lethargy of those who are its carriers could be prevented. In more than 20 years of an intensive and unique learning experience (nominally as president of the Committee for Economic Development [CED]), I must have learned something that should be preserved. Porter McKeever, then president of the JDR 3rd Fund, agreed and helped persuade three foundations to join with the JDR 3rd Fund in financing the small out-of-pocket cost of writing this book. They were the Ford Foundation, the Alfred P. Sloan Foundation, and the Edna McConnell Clark Foundation. My thanks go to all four.

The book depended on access to the CED archives and files. The CED's executive committee, at the behest of Philip M. Klutznick, authorized my use of those largely unworked materials so long as there were no quotations or attributions to the persons whose views were used. Readers including those whose views were used, will appreciate how carefully that injunction has been followed.

The staff of the CED cooperated fully in making microfilmed and file materials available and even in discovering sources that I had forgotten. I am especially indebted to Theodora Boskovic, assistant to the president of the CED, for both suggesting and locating obscure documents in the CED's custody that I had left in the files.

For research assistance, especially on Chapters 7 and 8, I am grateful to Arthur Rones of the Columbia University Graduate School. For her careful copyediting and typing of most of the final drafts, I am grateful to Norma Harrison.

Lyle C. Fitch, president of the Institute for Public Administration, Bernard L. Gladieux, consultant in public administration, and Robert F. Lenhart, former vice-president of the CED, made helpful comments and suggestions on Chapter 8.

Philip M. Klutznick, who initiated the writing process, was kind enough to conclude it with a gracious foreword as well as to offer helpful advice on the last chapter.

Finally, I express appreciation to my wife for her encouragement and enduring patience.

CONTENTS

Chapter   Page

1

INTRODUCTION

A group of Japanese top executives visited the United States recently to study adjustment to the changing age structure of their population. The leader made a surprisingly familiar opening statement of his purpose:

> We don't want to discuss with you what we in Japanese business should be doing. Our agenda is what Japan should be doing and what the best policies are in the national interest. Only after we have thought through the right national policies, and have defined and publicized them, are we going to think about the implications for business and for our companies. Indeed we should postpone discussing economics altogether until we have understood what the right social policies are and what is best for the individual Japanese and for the country altogether. Who else besides the heads of Japan's large companies can really look at such a problem from all aspects? To whom else can the country really look for guidance and leadership in such a tremendous change as that of the age structure of our population?[1]

Almost 40 years before, a group of leading U.S. business executives were asked by the then secretary of commerce, Jesse Jones, to study how the U.S. economy could convert to a prosperous peacetime economy at the end of the war we had just entered. Business and government working together, he felt, could avoid the inflation and depression that had characterized the years immediately following the ends of earlier wars. The small group of business leaders founded what became the Committee for Economic Development (CED).[2]

During the occupation and reconstruction of Japan after the war, high officers in the occupation forces felt that the characteristic subservience of Japan's business leaders to their own pursuit of profits and to government direction

1

could be reformed by organizing a group similar to the CED in Japan. Such a group, the Keizai Doyukai, was formed and called itself, in English, the "CED of Japan." It became and still is, by common consent of top leadership, the number-two economic organization in Japan after Keidanren, which is the number one. The Japanese executive just quoted was paraphrasing the CED statement of purpose shared by U.S. and Japanese CED groups who had been in close association for many years.

But neither country's business leaders invented the notion that good economic policies must draw upon the knowledge, experience, and observations of men of affairs. *Political economy*, in the broadest sense of the term, grew out of the concerns in earlier centuries of merchants, financiers, agriculturists, philosophers, and statesmen about government and private policies that would further the growth and prosperity of their countries. Economic policy, to borrow an expression, was and still is too important to be left only to economists and officials of government. This book attempts to return to the root sources for insights into the making of economic policy.

My own interest in this intellectual minefield has grown out of many years as a teacher and writer in economics; as a member of a variety of governmental and private commissions, study groups, and development projects; as a central banker; and as head of the U.S. CED. The CED brought together persons from several of the most relevant learned professions and persons of affairs – business and other executives – who were dedicated to the study of how public policies could better advance the country's welfare and with it the fortunes not only of the organizations they directed but of the people of the country.

In the course of this work, the participants encountered major ideological conflicts among government and private economists and other social scientists as well as among the business, financial, and government executives involved.

Identification and analysis of the preconceptions that underlie these conflicts of views among parties to policy making constitute a minimal part of the professional work of economists and are largely unknown to executives. Much of the response to the intellectual dilemmas they encountered has culminated in a polarization of groups, not in the resolution of problems. Big business has subsidized institutes and professionals whose views are closest to its own (without examining too closely many unexpressed implications of the views of their professional allies), and universities and other centers of research have been closing ranks to strengthen their positions in the ideological conflicts that are becoming more evident and more intense. Public reaction has been loss of confidence in the principal actors: leaders in business, higher education and social science research, and government itself.

The present study cannot resolve the conflicts in policy making that plague Western society; neither can it properly incorporate the Eastern dimensions of the problem. Its purpose is to identify, to describe, to fix within the relevant structure of thought, and, above all, to explain the causes of the conflicts in policy making that emanate from disparate assumptions, structures of thought, and occupational imperatives of the various parties engaged in the process. As Edwin Land — a scientist and a business executive — said recently, "It is the infusion of models extraneous to a field into the established structures of that field that is the likely cause of the regeneration and transformation of the field."[3] I hope he is right.

WHAT MAKES THIS BOOK DIFFERENT?

What makes this study different from others is that it is based heavily on transcripts of discussions covering a wide range of issues by various parties involved in making policy recommendations in committees of the CED for almost 40 years. In this period more than 100 policy studies were produced and issued by committees of business and other executives who publicly acknowledged responsibility for them, except as reservations or dissents were noted in the studies. These policy statements were on subjects deemed to be of such importance that they were worthy of the effort. Individual studies often extended over two or three years, and some, like those on inflation and stabilization, were repeated periodically because the problems persisted.

One constraint in using these materials was that the ideas and arguments could be used but not by direct quotation or attribution; such restricted use of transcripts of CED discussions in this book has been authorized for the first time. A second, and self-imposed, constraint was to omit many of the issues discussed that were of short-lived interest or that were treated only in terms of the conventional wisdom of the professional drafters with which the participating executives took little exception.

Because the CED utilized a process that for many years was almost unique, some description of it might enhance understanding of this book.

SELECTION OF IMPORTANT SUBJECTS

The subjects to be studied were chosen by a continuing (but also continually renewed) small group of business executives and professional social scientists associated with universities and research institutions. There are good reasons why the process of selecting subjects was delegated to a small group of trustees and advisers. Some of those reasons are revealed in intermittent inquiries to the trustee executives asking for their rating of the relative importance of subjects on the agenda and for suggestions of additions. An inquiry addressed to all trustees at the end of 1971, just before the outbreak of the worst inflationary period in peacetime (a disturbance accentuated by the energy crisis), reveals some strengths and weaknesses in the prognostications of executives.

In the 1971 inquiry, inflation and related government fiscal policies were ranked of high importance both for the immediate future and for five to ten years ahead — a forecast that was right on target. Ranked high also for five to ten years ahead was the issue of improving productivity, a problem that grew increasingly important in the decade.

But inexplicably the subject of fuel and energy supplies was rated, at the end of 1971, next to lowest in importance on a list of 15 both for the next two years and for the next five to ten years, despite the considerable number of trustee executives in the energy industry. The energy crisis was simply not foreseen by almost all of those closest to the industry and, of course, by most research people as well. A crash program of study had to be developed to make up for this astonishing myopia. It should be noted in passing, however, that attention had been diverted by the outrage of business executives and many economists over the Club of Rome's challenging study — *The Limits to Growth*.[4]

Equally neglected in 1971 was the economic and social impact of the then-new broadcast media — cable television and satellite and laser transmission — which by the end of the decade were revolutionizing the whole communications industry. This subject was rescued only with foundation support.

A similar inquiry to trustee executives in mid-1977 also produced surprises. Trustee executives gave first importance for the next decade to reform of retirement systems but ranked low the problem of growth of government in the economy. On the whole, however, the issues that were ranked high in importance reflected judgments that are hard to fault: technology policy, inflation control, energy supplies, and long-term performance of the economy. On balance, the concentration of topic selection in a seasoned group of executives and advisers probably worked better than the periodic opinion polls of executives.

Each selected study was directed toward formulation of private and government policies that might be expected to alleviate or remedy major problems that impeded growth and productivity in the economy and therefore slowed growth in living standards — goals that were accepted almost without question as being desirable. Learned background papers and informed discussion were the principal inputs from which conclusions and recommendations were finally drawn after numerous discussions by committees of executives and professional advisers. The latter had no vote on the final outcome.

HOW CED STUDIES WERE ORGANIZED

For each subject on the CED agenda (10 to 12 was the usual number), a trustee chairman and a preparatory committee of 15 to 30 other trustees were appointed. Knowledge of and interest in the subject and a reasonable diversity of economic interests were important qualifications for membership, although there was a strong tradition as well as a bylaw requirement that the principle guiding each member must be the public interest, not that of any particular industry or segment of society. (Private interest could be expressed in signed footnotes to final reports and often was.)

The study committee selected a project director from in house or outside as well as a varied number of advisers from the fields of knowledge that were deemed most relevant.

Each study committee developed or adopted its own mode of operation. From observation it is possible to classify the principal modes used. This classification is my own and may not be concurred in by other observers.

MODES USED IN PREPARING POLICY STUDIES

Mode 1 was the initial full draft or the tour de force. The outstanding characteristic of this mode was that the project director, after a preliminary meeting or two of the subcommittee, which established limits for the study and some of the key issues to be included, undertook to prepare a full rough draft of a proposed policy statement, which was presented to the committee for discussion. This mode is premised upon a considerable amount of intellectual capital on the subject being in possession of the project director and advisers as well as the executives. When this method was used successfully, the rough draft was discussed and revised in two or three meetings of the subcommittee and presented to the full Research and Policy Committee of about 60 trustees, which approved, disapproved, or modified the draft.

The record of failure of this mode was relatively high. There are good reasons. The intellectual approach of the project director, which often represented only one of competing schools of thought, was often at variance with the preconceptions of the majority of the study committee. Without considerable discussion by the group and its advisers, the project director had only his intellectual capital and clairvoyance as guides. Moreover, the project director was sometimes inept in style and presentation; his draft often resembled a textbook more than it did a consensus statement. If the project director was inflexible and insensitive, his first draft would be the last that he was invited to present.

Mode 1, although characterized by a high risk of rejection, when successful was of high quality and low cost. Its chances of success were best when the policy statement was on a subject for which there was a fairly good intellectual discipline — for example, fiscal policy for the next federal budget or consolidation of local governments. It worked well when the project director was experienced and worked within the bounds of a well-established intellectual discipline without schisms among the sachems or the strong original views of the chairman of the group. It is my impression that most foundation-financed private study groups use this mode or Mode 3.

Mode 2 might be called partial drafting by stages. It had two distinct variants.

Mode 2A was used in a well-developed field of knowledge. In this variant the subcommittee defined the issues and the bounds with help from a project director and advisers. The first meeting or two of the subcommittee supplied background information and raised questions — for example, in an issues paper often prepared by a special "brains trust." The project director either wrote or commissioned papers to fill gaps in knowledge. These papers were presented and discussed. The project director drafted sections of a proposed policy statement on the basis of the subcommittee discussions and background papers, presenting partial drafts at successive meetings of the subcommittee until the statement was finally integrated and finished.

This mode was one of moderate cost and was effective where the knowledge requirement was coupled with some experience in this type of work by the project director. Mode 2A, the staged draft, was perhaps the most common method used for policy statements prepared on broad subjects such as national and international economic policy.

The alternative version of the second mode, Mode 2B, was used when knowledge was obtainable but was dispersed among fields of specialization. This variant of the staged draft was characterized by a step-by-step buildup of a policy statement on the basis of background papers, many of an original nature. In this mode, as in most, the subcommittee defined the major issues and bounds of the project, usually with heavy input by the project director and advisers. On most issues using this mode the project director commissioned background papers from members of different disciplines who pulled together the relevant material. As papers were completed, they were presented to the subcommittee, usually by their authors. The project director prepared a draft statement based upon the papers and the subcommittee's discussion, revising the draft for subsequent meetings and adding new material as it became available. This process was continued until a policy statement was completed or the subcommittee abandoned the project. In the latter event, the background papers were often edited and published in the names of the authors who took full responsibility for their content.

The third mode was the research-based draft. This mode was employed where knowledge was not well developed and organized and when it was essential to the preparation of a policy statement to fill gaps by acquisition of knowledge from further research in depth, often using questionnaires or interviews. Mode 3 is at the other end of the spectrum from Mode 1 in which the intellectual capital is available and the field of knowledge well defined. Once the often-extensive research was completed, Mode 3 employed a process like that described in Mode 2B.

The research-based mode was probably the most expensive and time-consuming of those employed. (Chapter 5 on social responsibilities was largely derived from a five-year project using it.) There were usually long lags between the subcommittee's opening meetings and its later ones because of the time required to collect data and make the studies that were an essential input to the project. The subcommittees were usually aware of the risks involved in this path-breaking mode and sometimes dropped the subject without regret and without a large cost when the project appeared not to be feasible.

There was a fourth mode, Mode 4, used for international studies involving U.S. and foreign groups, which, for the record, is contained in a note because it is not central to the subjects treated in this book.[5]

The foregoing represents only a rough and minimum classification of the modes of policy statement preparation that have been employed by the CED in recent decades. In its earliest years much more of the work was done by the Research and Policy Committee itself, which was then very small. Also, in the very early years much more of the work was based upon a so-called research study by an eminent scholar detailing the state of knowledge. His work was studied and discussed and provided the background for a policy statement. Mode 1 was used often for the early statements.

It might be concluded that time and expense could have been saved by concentrating heavily on the first mode and the first variant of the second mode. It should be noted, however, that the use of these two modes is appropriate and involves acceptable risks only for subjects meeting the knowledge conditions required. In recent years, some of the older problems — such as application of the stabilization budget policy — that met the knowledge requirements of the first mode have become less dominant and newer problems — such as quality of the environment, welfare reform, and national health care — that do not meet the knowledge conditions have become much more urgent.

It is clear that the CED had a wide range of choice in the selection of its processes but that choice was greatly influenced by the kinds of problems that it decided to address.

Whatever the mode used, the procedure followed to adopt a completed statement, being governed by written rules, was essentially the same. The preparatory committee, when it considered its study completed, presented it to the 60-person continuing Research and Policy Committee, usually in one or two meetings. Sometimes a study was sent back to the drawing board, occasionally a study was rejected, but usually the study was adopted subject to incorporation of changes proposed and accepted by the Research and Policy Committee. The revised draft was sent out for a vote by members of the Research and Policy Committee, each member having the right to incorporate in it personal comments of reservation or dissent.

EMPHASIS ON CONTRIBUTIONS TO UNDERSTANDING

The foregoing discussion of modes and procedures has another purpose here. It provided much of the basis used for the selection of problems to be treated in this book by the use of transcripts, particularly the subject matter in Chapters 3, 4, 5, and 6 and parts of Chapters 2 and 7. Most of the material in these chapters grew out of discussions and policy statements that employed Mode 2B, dispersed knowledge and draft by stages, or Mode 3, the research-based draft. These were the modes employed for major problems about which knowledge was uncertain and trustee-executive discussions were a major input and had a predominent influence in the drafting of the policy statements. The subjects treated by these modes in these chapters could not easily be handled by "received doctrine" in the professional literature because such literature either gave little clear direction or even pointed in directions that executives found unacceptable in terms of their own knowledge and philosophy. These are the conditions that promise a large substantive contribution to knowledge.

A substantial contribution to understanding can be made by discussions of problems that did not enjoy consensus either among professionals or between them and executives. There were many insights in the reasoning put forward during discussions that permitted a consensus to be reached by executives even when the learned advisers remained in dissent, divided, or took leave of the project. This book concentrates on such cases. It also adds material of my own and some executive views expressed in other forums. This is particularly true of the second chapter, on development of the U.S. economy, and the last chapter, on oligopolistic power and the role of executives of large companies in the government's own policy-making process.

The book incorporates views and arguments of executives of larger companies that may be surprising to many readers and that may raise questions about how representative their views may be. The two histories of the CED cite numerous examples of disagreement between the CED's published policy positions and the contemporary views of other business leaders and groups.[6] It is regrettable that, in part because of my own selection of subjects, the views of executives used in this book were not widely held in the executive corps at the time they were expressed. But there is ample basis for the judgment that those views are likely to be more acceptable now than they were at the time. The context usually provides a guide to contrary positions both within the CED group and with other parts of the business community.

MOTIVATIONS OF EXECUTIVES IN SEARCH OF TRUTH

To this point I have failed to answer an important question that by now must have occurred to the reader. It was asked in one form by the French head of a leading international intergovernmental institution at a dinner in his honor given by the CED's Executive Committee. His inquiry was both French and rhetorical. "I cannot," he said, "understand you successful American business executives. Just when you have achieved a position that would allow you to enjoy life with an actress or some such friend, you devote your energies instead to pursuing the public interest."[7]

It is not enough to answer that the CED's founders were asked to prepare the way for restoring a prosperous economy at the end of World War II as a service to their country. The motivation of generations of executives over a period of 40 years cannot rest upon that initial impetus.

Like all such questions, there is no simple answer. Some like the recognition and admission to membership in a rather exclusive club. Some found an outlet for genuine intellectual concerns that a busy career had not provided. Several trustees have declared, independently, that the CED was the college or graduate school that helped to assuage their thirst for knowledge in a lifetime of learning.

Fundamentally, most executives of large companies would probably agree that the health and growth of the economy were essential to the growth and profitability of their own businesses. But their interest was based on more than that. The trustee executives of the CED — especially those who worked on policy statements — were deeply devoted to the system of which they were a part. High employment was the basis for a strong economy and growing markets. Inflation, recession, and excessive unemployment endangered the continuance of the system. Poverty and slums advertised major failures of the system; it was believed that these conditions should not readily be accepted but instead must be eradicated to the extent that means could be found to do it. The inability of the system to bring a satisfying life to a large number of people posed the danger of increased government intervention, higher taxes, and possible undermining of the private enterprise market system that provided the foundation of corporate enterprises that the executives directed. These beliefs clearly motivated and energized most of the hard-working, forward-looking core group of trustees who kept the CED going and whose discussions and statements form the basis of this book. But there was a deeper reason for some.

As you will read in subsequent pages, most trustee executives did not believe that concentrating on their own businesses would, despite their best efforts, automatically maintain a healthy economy. Most probably hoped that would be so, but they knew that the federal government's monetary, fiscal, and tax policies; its national defense posture and defense expenditures; its international trade and investment policies; and its programs to underwrite retirement, health care, welfare, and social equity would greatly influence the level of the economy and their own company's results and would foster a widely held commitment to a social order in which they could operate successfully. For these reasons, most trustee executives of large companies resented the antagonistic relationship between big business and government that seemed to prevail in party politics and in Washington, D.C.

Beyond the preceding explicit and adequate rationalizations for their behavior, there were some who felt, and sometimes articulated, an uneasiness that the orderly, information-based, and often scientific ways of thinking and decision making that they practiced as executives of companies (often larger than many national governments) seldom seemed to have counterparts in public policy making about economic affairs. They did not argue that government should be run like a large corporation, but they equally recoiled from the notion that large corporations did or should operate as though they were in the mindless world envisaged in the philosophy or model of laissez-faire. Faced with so intractable an intellectual contradiction, many chose to go the route of seeking better control, by joint efforts where necessary, over those powers and functions of government that were most important to the continuity and to the success of their corporate operations in serving their perceived corporate constituencies. This is a thesis that surfaces in many places in the following pages, a thesis that is finally addressed head-on in the last chapter.

I cannot conclude these introductory observations without disclosing why a policy-making process that combines academic, professional, and government expertise with business acumen is likely to be better than others that do not employ that combination. Academic and professional people are highly skilled in formulating policy alternatives in a kind of game that employs the symbols, relationships, and intellectual constraints of their disciplines. The number of possible policy alternatives for resolving problems in social science is limited only by the imagination of the scientists, which is high, or by conditions and assumptions that they impose to reduce the almost endless proliferation of possibilities in a world of uncertainty. Assumptions and conditions are the security blankets of the social scientist's mind. Policy-making executives are similarly constrained in their choices by considerations of goal acceptability and costs and benefits, as well as by considerations of organizational capability, public acceptance, and effective leadership needed to initiate and carry out policy decisions. The interplay of all of these inputs to the policy-making process is seldom explicit, but the interaction of good minds employing their intellectual capabilities is, I am convinced, the basis for much better policy making than we have had. It is the description and analysis of such interactions over many years, and the consequences of the policies resulting from that process, that constitute the main stuff of this book.

NOTES

1. Quoted by Peter F. Drucker, "Learning from Foreign Management," *Wall Street Journal*, June 4, 1980.

2. See Karl Schriftgiesser, *Business Comes of Age* (New York: Harper, 1960), chap. 1.

3. Edwin Land, *A House for the American Academy of Arts and Sciences* (Lincoln, Mass.: Cambria Press, 1979).

4. Donella H. Meadows, Dennis L. Meadows, Jørgen Randers, and William W. Behrens III, *The Limits to Growth: A Report for the Club of Rome's Project on the Predicament of Mankind* (New York: Universe Books, 1972).

5. Mode 4 was developed for joint studies with foreign counterparts. Various types of studies were undertaken in conjunction with counterpart organizations abroad. These studies were usually in fields where the problems were shared, the state of knowledge was good, and the main purpose of the effort was to seek policies that could be applied effectively in different countries or in their relations with each other.

There are three major variants of this mode.

A. A CED statement with comments by one or more foreign organizations taking exception to the U.S. views;

B. Parallel statements by one or more foreign counterpart organizations and one by the CED, published together and often at variance with each other; and

C. Joint statements by the CED and one or more foreign counterparts that were in general agreement but with footnotes of exception by the CED and by the counterparts.

The preparation of policy statements in any of the three variants of Mode 4 with counterparts was both time-consuming and expensive, roughly in increasing order from Mode

4A through 4C. The major advantages of Mode 4 were that most international policies, to be successful, required the cooperation of other countries and that failure to take into account the points of view of other countries made for bad policy.

6. Karl Schriftgiesser, *Business and Public Policy* (Englewood Cliffs, N.J.: Prentice-Hall, 1967); and idem, *Business Comes of Age*.

7. The omission of reference to women executives did not reflect their absence on the CED's roster of trustees.

2

NATIONAL ECONOMIC PLANNING—
BUSINESS AND GOVERNMENT

The introduction in Congress of the Humphrey-Javits bill — the Balanced Growth and Economic Planning Act of 1975 — expressed the deep concern of many thoughtful citizens about the apparent inability of the U.S. economy to absorb the disruption caused by the unforeseen domination of world oil supplies and prices by the Organization of Petroleum Exporting Countries (OPEC) and their confusion over the rampant inflation, combined with recession, that followed.

The bill, however, was quietly buried, having succumbed to a massive attack from business leaders and others, which, in turn, expressed the strength of their devotion to the principles of the market system and an ideology that called for a limited role of government in the economy.

The contents of the proposed bill and the reaction to it both reflected some basic misconceptions about the structure and functions of the U.S. economy. Because this book is dedicated to the question of how the economy's functioning can be improved, it is appropriate at the beginning to review with some care the country's economic evolution and the strong influence on its development of planning.

To a greater extent than most people even suspect, the United States is a product of political and economic planning — planning based upon combining new theories of political economy with the unique reality of a virtually empty continent, fabulously rich in resources and begging to be developed.

And the country was successfully developed to an extent that is still the envy of most of the world, but adaptation of the philosophical framework that accompanied and supported that development has failed to keep pace with its success. Over the last decade, nations that never embraced our philosophy about the role of government in the economy have surpassed the United States in growth, productivity, control of inflation, and, in some cases, per capita income.

To avoid misunderstanding, we must remind ourselves that national economic planning has to do with the ways of determining what and how much to produce; how resources are exploited, allocated, and organized to produce what is expected to be consumed; and how what is produced is distributed to or shared by the people of the country. Inasmuch as there is already a planned system — called the market system — for doing these major economic chores in the United States, consideration of alternative or improved plans can be limited to those consistent with the present system. (Socialist economic planning, under which most business and industry would be government owned and centrally controlled, is not a real alternative.)

What is not included in the plan that is presently in operation is the rate of growth of output and employment and the extent to which income distribution resulting from operation of the market system will be modified. These two functions are relatively new to U.S. economic evolution and by their nature call for the use of powers that lie within the scope of government. Because not everyone agrees what the *scope of government* is or should be, its present status deserves some analysis.

First, all governments make and carry out plans to provide public goods, that is, goods and services that are consumed in common by the whole population and that cannot be rationed to individuals by the price system. These include the basic structure of government itself (the legislative, executive, and judicial branches), national defense, law and order, public health, and basic education. This type of planning has almost universal support, at least in principle, and is constantly undergoing changes aimed at improvement.

Second, governments take positive measures in the private economy to increase the efficiency of the market system by establishing standards for weights, measures, grades, commercial codes, traffic regulations, and the like. Provision of a monetary unit as a standard of value also belongs on this list. To be sure, this type of activity can be overdone; nevertheless, a considerable amount is necessary to make the market system work smoothly without constant recourse to conflict or to the courts.

Third, governments provide essential services that would be inadequately supplied by the market. They subsidize or even exercise ownership of certain sectors that are crucial but not self-supporting from charges: the U.S. Postal Service, Conrail and Amtrak, and the tax-supported federal highway system. These cases represent pragmatic intervention to provide essential services; they do not reflect any basic ideological considerations.

Fourth, government provides assistance for particular types of economic activity to encourage private interests to devote more resources to developments that have consequences for the country as a whole beyond what private interests can supply on a paying basis: special tax treatment for exploration or development of new energy sources and tax credits for investment in new equipment, DISC (the Domestic International Sales Corporation), and the like.

These activities raise mainly the issue of whether the incentives accomplish their purpose in the most cost-effective way, given any alternatives that might prevail. They affect the allocation of resources but represent a form of partial planning that is generally acceptable to business leaders and the government, albeit they do not constitute an alternative economic system that might supplant the market system.

Fifth, governments impose negative restraints on various types of business through law and regulation to affect the allocation of resources and the operation of firms in the market. Most negative regulation is for the purpose of protecting the people from menaces to public health and safety, or excessive monopoly power (for example, by regulation of public utilities), or other cases where the market system is unable to provide adequate protection of service. By and large, such regulation is designed to make a market system more acceptable and more responsive to consumers. To make a plan based upon the market system work satisfactorily, there must be some degree of regulation of what the strong can do to the weak. The market system cannot function well without some regulation of its members.

The foregoing examples of government intervention are traditional means of improving the performance of a predominantly market system. To repeat, they are not intended to replace the system or to determine the overall level and rate of growth at which it operates. They moderate the height of the waves and the strength of currents in the market ocean; they do not materially affect its tides. Actions by governments to influence the growth of the economy and its stability are products of recent times and almost experimental, as they are now generally employed by the industrial democracies. The origins and workings of this type of planning will constitute a major element in this book, especially of Chapter 3.

Not included in the preceding list are government provisions for protection or relief to the individual from the hazards of poverty, sickness, or accident. These are centuries-old functions of government, but in recent years their expansion has constituted an almost revolutionary change in government responsibilities. Government's role in influencing the level of the economy and providing basic economic security for the individual is still evolving in form if not in substance.

VOLUNTARY BUSINESS PLANNING FOR HIGH POSTWAR EMPLOYMENT

Probably the most comprehensive short-term national planning effort of U.S. business, now generally forgotten, was that for postwar reconversion and full employment carried out in the closing years of World War II under the auspices of the Committee for Economic Development (CED). It consisted of two parts: postwar planning by and for individual firms throughout the country and national fiscal, monetary, and employment policies for high employment.

World War II began in 1939 with an unemployment rate of 16 percent, down somewhat from the level of 25 percent reached in the depth of the depression of

1929-33. The CED was organized in 1942 by a joint initiative of a group of business leaders, mostly in the Business Advisory Council, and the U.S. Department of Commerce to develop analyses and plans to prevent a depression after the war such as had occurred after most previous wars.

Business organized itself across the nation by city and community in about 3,000 places to take stock, company by company, of where it would be after the war. Postwar employment was estimated company by company, and firms facing dim prospects were helped (largely by voluntary actions) to develop new products and markets to take up the slack. Most large companies integrated their plans with those of suppliers, customers, and a target of high employment for the country as a whole. Transition programs for terminating war contracts and reconverting were worked out together with plans for public works, unemployment compensation, and education and retraining for workers.

Most important, this vast voluntary effort was a success. There was a high level of employment after the war. The CED's projection of total employment a year after the end of the war — necessarily crude because of being derived from a mass of company plans — was closer to the mark than any other responsible estimate. Why introduce this bit of history never since repeated? Because it provides a guide to the type of government-business cooperation in planning that might have some chance of success today. (The last chapters of this book will return to the subject.)

In the years since the end of World War II, emphasis on maintaining high employment has shifted almost entirely to the second type of high-employment planning: government fiscal, monetary and related macroeconomic policies, and unemployment relief and training programs. These have been vigorously and continuously supported by business leaders, although the government's record for these types of planning in recent years has not been outstanding.

The impression that business opposes national economic planning is derived largely from the reaction of a number of business leaders to the spate of planning bills introduced in Congress in recent years, particularly the Humphrey-Javits bill. The latter would have had the president present a detailed six-year economic plan to Congress for enactment into law; its purpose led many to swarm to its support. Subsequently, some supporters and most opponents were stung by recognition that adoption of a comprehensive national economic plan would unnecessarily destroy a system that has been gradually adopting those instruments of planning that are necessary to maintain high employment and would replace it with a huge boondoggle for the benefit of econometricians, politicians, and civil servants. Is it not, therefore, worth a little study of how the unique economic system of this country came to be and why national economic planning in the United States should develop from that unique base to be effective?

THE ROOTS OF PLANNING IN U.S. ECONOMIC HISTORY

Today's antagonism to national economic planning (regardless of the meaning intended) has its roots in the country's economic development and the philosophical concepts that paralleled it. The American Revolution was in considerable measure a revolt against a type of plan that reflected the mercantilist ideas and practices of the mother country, England, which attempted to guide and control colonial development from a faraway center of power.

The revolution did not, however, stamp out the concept of planned economic development. The last act of the Continental Congress was the Ordinance of 1787, which provided for the Northwest Territory to be surveyed, settled, and organized first as territories and then as states — a pattern that was followed in other areas as the country expanded. Through most of the nineteenth century, the federal government pursued an activist policy based on a plan to settle and develop outlying regions. The plan was coherent, even if not defined in detail.

The government's greatest asset was land, which, although often subject to titles originally granted by foreign governments and Indian tribes (usually in that order) was opened to settlement on progressively easier terms until, with the Homestead Act in 1862, it became available to settlers in 160-acre tracts merely by occupancy and improvement.

The key to land-based prosperity was transportation — movement to markets of products of the developing farms, forest industries, and mines. Federal, state, and local governments throughout the nation's history have participated in authorizing and financing road and canal building, waterway improvement, and construction of railroads and, more recently, a network of federal highways, airways, and communications. These supplied the arteries for selling and transporting products to markets and the means to haul westward from eastern and foreign factories the goods, tools, and people needed for exploiting the country's resources. However this system was planned, it depended basically upon a federal government that made lands and rights to exploitation and development available for private use and provided protection through a system of defense, law, and justice that only government can supply.

But all government activity was not confined to providing land, infrastructure, and order. The seaboard states of the East saw their farmers migrate to lands that they themselves had ceded earlier to the federal government, and they observed a steady increase in imports of competing goods from foreign countries. Having experienced the pinch of control over commerce by the mother country, eastern merchants and manufacturers had become acquainted with the advantage of tariffs and understood that customs and excises were and would be for a long time the main sources of central government revenues that were needed to pay for defense, infrastructure, and justice. Tariff protection was accorded infant industries (but usually continued after they grew up). Since the South trended toward agricultural development, until the latter part of the nineteenth century the North turned out to be the principal beneficiary of tariff protection. The tariff became a mainstay of industrial development and remained so well into the present century.

The productive system of the nation and its commerce depended upon money and credit, which only a central government can plan and regulate.

Herein lay what was probably the nation's worst planning failure, partly because the principles of central banking were unknown for a long time but largely because the government failed to recognize that its monetary authority was indispensable and should be supreme. A good start was made with the Bank of the United States chartered in 1816 by the federal government; but after the bank lost its charter in 1836, the country lapsed into makeshift arrangements until well into this century.

The essentials of a plan for the nation's development were recognized and articulated by many political leaders in the first half of the nineteenth century. The most succinct was Henry Clay's "American System," the keys to which were "the [central] Bank, the Tariff and Internal Improvements."

The country's development also depended upon education, recognized first by the Northwest Ordinance, which encouraged free public education and reserved lands in each township for schools, later by land grants for colleges provided by the Morrill Act of 1862, and today by enormous amounts of federal aid for education and stringent requirements for equal educational opportunities.

Development of the United States according to the rough-hewn plan just described was a unique experience that molded the character of Americans in ways well described by Frederick Turner.[1] It also produced a rate of growth and prosperity in the course of two centuries that almost boggles the mind. Solomon Fabricant has summarized the results in a bicentennial essay.

> Today's [1976] population . . . is 85 times the population estimated for 1776. Today's [1976] real product or income per person is about 18 times the level at about the time of the Revolution. Total product [GNP] . . . multiplied 1500 times over the 200-year period. . . . Over the past 200 years, the volume of goods and services per person in the population doubled every 50 years on the average.[2]

THE RISE AND FALL OF LAISSEZ-FAIRE

The economic development of the United States is again unique in that it was paralleled by acceptance of a laissez-faire doctrine that was spread widely in Adam Smith's *Wealth of Nations*, published the year that the American Revolution began. A system depending on private enterprise and the market was readily accepted in the United States: keep enterprise open; let the market determine what is produced and the prices, wages, and profits that result from production; and confine government to defense, justice, and public works (to which, as a home-grown adjunct, we added education and then, as a corruption, tacked on tariff protection). Most Americans, however, do not appreciate that England and the United States were almost alone in adopting this system as the basis of their economies. The attempt to export their economic credo was less successful than the results they themselves achieved by using it at home.

The natural tendency toward monopoly under laissez-faire was curbed by the conspiracy doctrine in the common law, which proved to be especially effective against unions but eventually (and fully in accord with the spirit of the system) became the basis of antitrust laws applied to industrial and other monopolies The laissez-faire economy provided a form of planning that suited the development of a continental-sized country, and it did not lack monitoring by intellectuals, lawyers, judges, and elected officials.

From today's perspective, laissez-faire can be viewed as having had some insuperable weaknesses. Inasmuch as the doctrine has had an intellectual revival, and has instinctive appeal to business leaders, it is well to consider some of those weaknesses.

Its major theoretical flaw is that the whole was not recognized as being capable of being either greater or less than the sum of the parts, the differences being the money supply and its activity and international capital movements. As fractional reserve banking became increasingly important by issuance of paper currency and by bank loans, and as the United States had no central bank as a lender of last resort from 1836 to 1914, the economy was subject to financial crises. Other sources of financial instability, improperly foreseen, were the effects of international capital movements in a world of liberal trade and convertible currency. The currency instability — liquidity crises and a roller coaster of price inflations and deflations — of the United States and other countries in the eighteenth and nineteenth centuries was probably tolerable to business people and investors. Such persons could denominate contracts in secure British pounds sterling and maintain London bank balances no matter what happened to their domestic money. They could also hold gold or silver.

Other flaws were inherent in the English elitism in which laissez-faire was nurtured. Adam Smith and his followers ignored or rejected the possibility of universal free education and universal suffrage. In the United States the first became almost an article of religion, and the second was largely attained for white males by the middle of the nineteenth century — in some states, long before. Literacy and the vote led inexorably to demands for the political redress of economic ills. One is tempted to suggest that a little education was bound to lead to the rejection of laissez-faire except as it was preserved as an intellectual tool by economists and others of the intelligentsia.

Perhaps Smith's most inexcusable flaw was to denigrate the corporation to the role of being capable of performing only routine functions requiring large capital — undertakings such as canals, waterworks, and turnpikes. Royal corporate charters had for centuries been sought for all kinds of ventures, including the colonization of America. For a canny Scot to ignore the possibility of generalizing a privilege that had demonstrated its value to business was to ignore what became one of the most important instruments for development — an instrument so effective that it became the object of an enormous amount of legislation and regulation.

Of course Smith and his followers could not have foreseen the emergence of the Third World (safely colonial for the most part in the nineteenth century and until the end of World War I) or control of the bulk of the world's developed energy supplies, and much of its mineral raw materials, by countries that had never heard of laissez-faire or, if they had, were determined to have as little of it as possible.

As laissez-faire in the United States matured, it required more and more patching up. The railroads became oppressive and discriminatory and had to be regulated (Interstate Commerce Commission [ICC], 1887) as to rates and other practices for almost a century. Public utilities were recognized as similar to railroad monopolies in their heyday and were regulated by the states. The trusts — large industrial and commercial firms having monopolistic power — became unconscionably predatory, not only against consumers but (unforgivably) against competitors. The first federal antitrust law (the Sherman Act) initiated a procession of remedial measures after 1893, followed by much other legislation in succeeding decades. The monetary system was finally put on a single standard — originally gold — and the Federal Reserve System (supplementing the inadequate system set up by the National Banking Act) brought the banks under better supervision and gave some needed elasticity to the money supply. Unions gained legal status in the courts and were finally (in 1932) given clear federal legal protection.

THE GREAT DEPRESSION — AND THE END OF LAISSEZ-FAIRE?

A great surge of economic growth during and after the Civil War enabled the pragmatic patchwork of laissez-faire to keep going until it broke apart at the seams during the Great Depression of 1929-32. It was still being mended at the outbreak of World War II.

There was nothing in the laissez-faire plan to provide guidance for recovering from a great depression like that of the 1930s. Following instincts in keeping with the system, business executives cut production, laid off workers, cut wages, and even slashed prices without stopping the slide that started with a financial panic in 1929. Banks called loans and saw their borrowers declare bankruptcy; then many closed their doors. Farmers lost their farms and countless people lost their homes in foreclosures. The country had survived financial panics and depressions in earlier times when the economy was simpler and urban/industrial workers could go back to the farms to weather the storm. Now the farm itself had become commercial and had entered its own depression even sooner than the rest of the economy; farmers' children had migrated to industrial centers and the cities. The nation was sacrificed not on William Jennings Bryan's cross of gold but on a stubbornly held outmoded philosophy, which is still influential in the rhetoric of some politicians and business executives.

There being no economic plan to end the depression of the 1930s (but the one then bankrupt), pure pragmatism and much bad theory eventually took over. Farmers and homeowners were bailed out by hastily passed legislation.

Banks that had not failed were shored up with emergency loans or take-overs, and deposit insurance was mandated. The Federal Reserve, not yet fully aware of its central banking responsibility, was unable to restore the money supply for want of suitable collateral for loans to banks that would enable them to extend adequate credit. It was eventually authorized to make loans on government securities or any sound asset, and the Reconstruction Finance Corporation was created to bail out the banks; but these actions came too late. As state and local governments ran out of money to pay welfare bills, the federal government took over the burden. Public works and public emergency employment programs were established to relive unemployment. Ultimately, in 1937 the Social Security system was established and from the beginning provided benefits for the needy aged. An unemployment insurance system was instituted but was of little benefit to those already unemployed.

The emergency measures just described, undertaken out of sheer necessity, were accompanied by other desirable long-run reforms. Securities markets and securities issuance were regulated. Banks were brought under better regulation, forced to get out of the business of securities issuance, and required to insure deposits with the Federal Deposit Insurance Corporation up to a reasonable limit per depositor. The Federal Housing Administration-insured amortizing mortgage was invented and made available, replacing the financing of homes by demand or short-term loans and eventually bringing more than 60 percent of the country's families into home ownership, thus establishing a strong bulwark for private ownership. Farmers producing major crops (wheat, corn, and cotton) were given protection against disastrously low prices, and new institutions were introduced to provide long- and short-term farm credit. Labor unions obtained the right to organize and bargain collectively with the support of the federal government and the courts. This is, of course, only a partial list of New Deal reforms — all without evaluation.

The profusion of emergency and reform measures adopted to cope with the Great Depression signalized that for the first time, and without any coherent plan, the federal government had assumed responsibility for the overall performance of the economy, for the nation's levels of employment and national income. The laissez-faire plan no longer could be trusted to meet these overriding needs.

Some of the reforms implied much more. Laissez-faire was no longer to have responsibility for provision of adequate credit, for truth in securities issuance or conduct of securities or commodities markets, for minimum farm prices, or for looking after the unemployed, the aged, and the indigent. By the end of the 1930s, the federal government not only had taken over a lion's share of responsibility for the economy's aggregate performance but also had given a large measure of assurance that everyone could expect a minimum level of personal economic security. Both changes were or could be made consistent with a market economy and, in principle, are generally supported today, even by business.

World War II finally swept away unemployment in a rushing tide of production — a tide that floated all the stranded boats not beyond repair.

The wartime performance taught two important lessons, now but dimly remembered. The first was that under emergency conditions the economy could be planned for enormous productivity, so long as the system was centrally directed, goals were established, and the government assisted business to meet them. At the peak as much as 40 percent of the nation's output was diverted to the war effort.

The second lesson was that sufficiently strong aggregate demand, if accompanied by drafting people into the armed services and allocating materials and finance as well as setting wage and price controls, could virtually eliminate unemployment. Totalitarian (war) economies abroad in the prewar period demonstrated the same capacity. Few would wish to resort to war or dictatorship as a means of achieving full employment, but we have yet to obtain a consensus on an alternative that is consistent with individual freedom. The search for that alternative continues as the economy rocks under buffets from a succession of recessions that have not cured a continuing inflation.

GOVERNMENT'S NEW ROLE AS
STABILIZER OF THE ECONOMY

The CED's first crop of business executive trustees determined to draw the right lessons for the future from depression and wartime experiences. They were assisted (sometimes in the wrong direction) by a group of social scientists who were, for the most part, nondoctrinaire learners from the same experiences. Their remarkably successful planning effort for liquidating war production and speedy reconversion has already been described. They were equally determined to find ways of attaining and maintaining high employment and rising living standards in a peacetime economy, not only in the United States but in postwar Europe and Japan and, ultimately, in the rest of the world.*

The CED's first crop of trustees was aware that planning in a peacetime economy was an unpopular notion. The National Resources Planning Board, organized in the period before our entry into World War II, was summarily abolished by Congress in early 1943, just after the CED went into business. The intellectual heirs of Adam Smith had their knives ready even for business executives who might take the planning route.

But new doctrines and new tools were available to the small band of business executives, social scientists, and political leaders who were determined to prevent another slide into the slough of depression after the war. One was

---

*The Economic Cooperation Administration that was of critical importance to Europe's postwar recovery was headed by Paul Hoffman, the CED's first chairman, and had numerous CED trustees as administrators.

the enormous influence of Keynesianism, which stressed macroeconomics and the determinants of aggregate employment and income. Another was the new, still current, statistical series of the Department of Commerce, cast in the macroeconomic mold, GNP and its components, including the dynamic elements of private investment, foreign trade, and government expenditures and revenues. The CED and a growing number of other groups had learned the lesson that the level of the economy would not take care of itself and that the federal government should take ultimate responsibility, working through both governmental and private instrumentalities, for maintaining a satsifactory level of employment and income.

At the end of the war these statements, which now seem so bland and noncontroversial, were revelations to some and heresy to others. During my many years at the CED and in the Federal Reserve System, I answered more questions about this last proposition than on any other subject. "How long," asked one of my Federal Reserve superiors just after World War II, "can the government run deficits before we [Federal Reserve] run out of money?"

The architects of the CED's postwar policies for high employment shrewdly founded their program on unassailable ground. This was that the primary instruments of a policy for stabilizing the economy should be incontrovertibly the instruments inherent in and controlled by the government itself. By this time — more than 150 years after the Constitution had originally reserved to Congress the right to create money and regulate its value — it was clear that the monetary authority and its instruments were qualified as instruments of planning. But even more important were the fiscal powers to tax and to appropriate money and to borrow on the government's credit. However independent the Federal Reserve might be, it could not supersede the government's fiscal authority nor its own responsibility to Congress.

Paul Hoffman, first chairman of the CED, testifying before the Senate Banking and Currency Committee in August 1945 in favor of what was to become the Employment Act of 1946, made the new philosophy clear. He first reaffirmed the businessman's faith in free enterprise, but he also asserted the new stabilizing role of government.

> The crucial role, the most vital function of government in fostering employment is, I am convinced, to establish conditions under which a free enterprise system can operate most effectively and to counteract the tendencies in the system toward booms and depressions.

He then enunciated the new responsibility of government, cast in terms of a businessman's understanding and without econometrics:

> The direct effect of the collection of taxes, of the expenditure of public funds, of the control of credit, and the indirect effect of the whole body of government fiscal and monetary policies on the confidence

of businessmen and individuals exerts perhaps the greatest leverage government has on [levels of] production and employment.[3]

At the time, representatives of other groups of businessmen did not join him in supporting the Employment Act; most were vigorously opposed. The opponents, however, have passed from the scene and most of their successors are active participants in or followers of the discussions and testimony before the Joint Economic Committee of Congress and in other forums on economic stabilization.

In subsequent years, the CED spelled out its views on stabilizing budget policies, the role of monetary policy, emergency tax increases, and tax cuts. These are not subjects to be treated here. Of immediate importance is that, from the beginning in 1946, the CED's leaders never forgot that the government is made up of three branches, two being responsible for discharging the new duties of economic stabilization. The executive role was clear; a Council of Economic Advisers to the president had been created at the CED's suggestion to advise the president on the state of the economy and on budget policies required to discharge the stabilizing function. Further responsibility lay with Congress, which in the end disposed of the budget and with it most of the executive proposals.

In policy statements and testimony over a period of 30 years, the CED argued that Congress was not discharging its part of the government's stabilization responsibility. Except for the nonlegislating Joint Economic Committee, its committees did not consider the budget as a whole and the effect it would have on the economy. Finally, in the Budget and Impoundment Control Act of 1974, Congress made a change in its procedures even more significant than in the act of 1921, which mandated the first budget for the federal government. Congress established a joint budget committee of both houses and a budget committee for each to set limits for the budget as a whole, taking into account its effect on the economy. Appropriations and finance committees and subcommittees had to stay within guidelines prescribed by a joint resolution or secure an amendment to the joint resolution for permissible deviations. In the name of economic stabilization, fiscal responsibility had been imposed by Congress upon itself — an act that, if it prevails, will represent a historic constitutional reform. (If it does not prevail, we shall all live in economic chaos.) Moreover, budget targets and their effects on the economy are projected five years ahead, subject to annual updating.

Whether the American people realize it or not, national economic planning for high employment through government fiscal and monetary processes has arrived. And it has strong business and public support. What remains to be determined is whether planning by means of monetary and fiscal policies will be enough, especially if each is free to offset the other. But it should be remembered that the budget part of the plan was put into place in its present form not in 1946 by the Employment Act but in 1975, nearly 20 years later.

In recent decades, business interest and participation in planning have not been limited to the national economy. In states, cities, and towns, business has been an active participant in regional and local planning for transportation, urban renewal, economic development, pollution control, parks and recreation, schools, housing, and a host of other problem areas. As changes that are deemed desirable have encountered obstacles in the form of inadequate state and local government structures and finances, business interest in reforms of government organization and processes has grown. All over the country thousands of school districts have been consolidated. In many places local governments have been reorganized or brought into more effective cooperation as partners in metropolitan governments or coalitions of local governments. Business groups have been active in a great many of these efforts and have obtained good experience from working with governments at all levels.

GOVERNMENT'S NEW ROLE IN PLANNING – AND ITS FLAWS

The new fiscal-monetary process for stabilizing the economy is a form of national economic planning for high employment without inflation. It is a form of planning consistent with the kind of market economy that we have or at least would like to have. And, as we shall see, it requires little additional authority from new legislation. The process was buttressed by the Humphrey-Hawkins Act in 1977, which calls for the president to establish each year a comprehensive set of national economic goals and to reflect them in each year's budget. To that extent, Humphrey-Hawkins merely incorporates present practice. How much more will be spelled out respecting programs and policies needed to meet the announced goals remains to be seen.

Consider the elements already routinely included in this planning process. First, a projection must be made of what the economy would look like at *full employment* (as that term is defined) and without inflation or with a given rate of inflation. To make this projection, the GNP must be adjusted to include the increment that would be added by increasing the rate of employment, for additions to the labor force and for reducing unemployment to the desired level. Then, the levels of tax revenue at existing rates and of government expenditures under existing and projected programs must be estimated. Unless the country is in a depression, or there are extraordinary capital needs implicit in the full employment GNP, the federal budget (on the national income and product account basis) should be in balance at the full employment level, remembering that this level should contain little or no inflation. Should new or increased government expenditure programs be undertaken that will throw the full employment budget into deficit, unless there is a depression, new tax revenues must be found or existing expenditure programs cut back to restore the balance.

We may take it for granted that with the data and models now available, the full employment GNP estimates will include breakdowns of gross domestic investment including inventory changes and housing, imports and exports and the trade balance, and consumer expenditures broken down into various classes of durable and nondurable goods and services. These major classifications may be further subdivided by industry or activity, using methods based on past data and relationships and current surveys of plans such as those for business capital expenditures, intentions of consumers to buy housing, automobiles, and other durable goods, and so forth. Even financing intentions for capital expenditures and durable consumer goods can be projected.

All of these estimates and projections are carried on within the staffs of the congressional budget committees, the Office of Management and Budget, the Council of Economic Advisers, and other agencies. They apply to a fiscal year that begins one year or more later and are embodied in a budget that is presented by the president early in the calendar year but not completed by Congress until its end (despite an October 1 deadline). Note, however, that the leading actors in the private sector of the economy, which accounts for almost three-quarters of the GNP, are not included in the process except as reporters of data. In fact, such plans as those for capital expenditures are made on whatever basis the private company uses, not on the basis of a given level of GNP, given tax rates, employment levels, and the like.

What is missing in the current process of making the national economic plan? A sharing of information and an interaction of ideas between government and the private sector and, in particular, assurance to the latter of the government's plans and targets. The one experiment in massive private sector planning that was described earlier and that was conducted at a time when data, models, and computers were scarce or not available demonstrated that private sector planning could produce results that turned out to be surprisingly better than those of government. It is the inability of government and private planners to work together that virtually dooms even the rudimentary form of national planning just described to intolerable ranges of error and leads people to support such drastic changes as those embodied in the Humphrey-Javits bill and the Humphrey-Hawkins Act.

Is this obvious flaw in the planning process correctable? It results partly from the lack of experience, inability, and antagonism of the parties on both sides. That adversary relationship stems mainly from misapplication of the market system's philosophy and the laws based upon it. Restrictions imposed by antitrust and conflict-of-interest laws, a variety of regulations, and other legal restraints make it difficult, if not impossible, for key business and industry representatives to join in discussions with government officials, to disclose their own plans for investment and employment, and to work with the government people toward developing realistic, consistent, attainable goals. Were it not for legal restrictions and some foot dragging on both sides, a basis for public-private cooperative planning would be possible. We witnessed it during World War II in the War Production Board, the Office of Price Administration, and subsequently in government commissions and private study groups in this country and abroad. It can be done within the market system.

As the closing chapter of this book will demonstrate, it is not necessary that thousands of business people be involved. The strategic elements in the private sector that will largely determine its level of employment, investment, and international trade can be represented by a few hundred persons. Until the obstacles to effective, voluntary national economic planning to achieve overall employment and investment goals can be hurdled, the government will continue to miss its targets at the cost of unnecessary unemployment and hundreds of billions of dollars in lost production. Continuing unsatisfactory performance of the economy probably is still the biggest threat to the market system, as it has been in the past. Cooperation from the private sector can be ensured by recognition of this danger by most leaders in business and government.

INTERNATIONAL ECONOMIC PLANNING AND NATIONAL POLICY

Planning in the United States never was and never can be limited to the domestic economy alone. The Constitution lodges international relations in the domain of the president, subject to Senate ratification of treaties. Historically, this made planning of international economic affairs a tidier process than planning of the home economy. In the immediate postwar period, the international economic agenda included the international monetary system, international trade, international investment, and, for a few years, reconstruction of the European and Japanese economies.

The main objectives for international money were at first clear: a return to convertible currencies at fixed exchange rates — the international counterpart of interregional use of domestic currency — and loans or grants for reconstruction to war-torn countries that could not restore currency convertibility because of their limited ability to earn foreign exchange. The pound sterling (which had been the world's key currency for more than a century before World War I) was supplanted by the dollar after World War II. The Bretton Woods agreements of 1944, which provided for an International Bank for Reconstruction and Development (IBRD) and an International Monetary Fund (IMF) for helping countries keep their international payments in balance, were supposed to achieve the monetary and reconstruction objectives. In fact, it was only after massive infusions of U.S. Marshall Plan aid and direct U.S. loans that in 1958 the leading industrial countries restored the principal elements of currency convertibility and fixed exchange rates, with the dollar continuing as the world's most important key currency. Then in 1971 the dollar — in deep difficulty because of substantial deficits in the U.S. balance of payments, which stemmed, in considerable measure, from the above grants and loans — was devalued. The system of fixed rates changed, step by step, to flexible or to managed floating-rate arrangements that are still in the process of transition.

International money and financial planning for the early years of the postwar period was not (considering the subsequent breakdown of the international monetary system set up at Bretton Woods) a great monument to successful planning. It did, however, provide the institutions and processes that, after successive adaptations and much delay, finally helped to keep the major currencies convertible, thus providing the vehicle to finance an enormous expansion in world trade and investment. As with domestic planning for high employment, the processes and political will to pursue sound objectives may have been more important than the institutions and plans themselves.

The plan for fixed exchange rates represented the conventional wisdom of bankers and finance ministers. In its purest form − a gold standard − it represented the ultimate in conservative economics (the right wing of laissez-faire), and still has advocates. Latter-day advocates of the gold standard wished mainly to protect the domestic economy from what they considered excessively large government-financed social programs by imposing the discipline of free convertibility of domestic money into gold, which could be shipped abroad out of reach of the reformers, to the accompaniment of deflation and unemployment in profligate countries. The gold standard is probably impractical because it requires governments to put themselves in a monetary straitjacket that frustrates their other objectives.

The plan for floating exchange rates, which would be free to move up or down with conditions of supply and demand in foreign exchange markets, rested upon the principle that if domestic prices, wages, or even public expenditures were for whatever reason to become so high that exports persistently fell short of imports and the deficit caused too much loss of foreign exchange reserves, then the balance could be redressed by allowing key foreign currency exchange rates with other countries to depreciate. This would reduce the foreign currency prices of exports, which would stimulate sales abroad, and raise the domestic currency prices of imports, which would make them less attractive.

Conversely, if a country's exchange rates were already too low (as with the Japanese yen and German mark for several years before the early 1970s), they could be allowed to appreciate, raising the foreign currency price of the appreciating country's exports and reducing the domestic currency price of its imports − an experience well known for a number of years to U.S. buyers of Volkswagens and Toyotas and even better appreciated by their foreign makers. Thus floating exchange rates became, in the eyes of those advocating free markets and social reformers alike, the answer to balance-of-payments losses attributable to pursuit of domestic expansionary economic policies at a more rapid pace than that of other industrial countries.

Something is missing from the floater's case. All countries in a worldwide recession, for example, cannot depreciate against all others. Many will intervene to prevent what they consider to be excessive depreciation of their currencies. Moreover, when balance-of-payments deficits result from increases by a cartel in the prices of imported oil, higher costs for foreign exchange may raise domestic prices of imported oil, but they will not necessarily be offset by increased imports by the foreign oil-producing countries whose domestic markets are too small to generate the volume of imports needed to restore the balance.

So far, foreign oil export surpluses have been recycled through financial markets back to the biggest oil importing countries: the United States, Japan, and Western Europe. In effect, the oil exporters have financed their own sales but not necessarily by lending to those who are in greatest need of financial aid: the developing countries that do not produce oil. Eventually, the financing of oil imports by developing countries must be planned and financed; to some extent this is already being done through international institutions. Meanwhile, large movements of OPEC foreign exchange balances, and other movements of capital, can cause erratic fluctuations in exchange rates, which give the wrong signals to governments and financial institutions as to the true state of a nation's balance of payments and competitive position. No less than under a fixed exchange rate system, the planning and management of exchange rates under flexible or floating rates in today's world cannot long be avoided by major industrial countries, including our own. Management of exchange rates in leading countries is now the common practice.

There is an analogy here to stabilizing domestic fiscal and monetary policies. If they are carried out well, government planning of production, prices, and wages becomes superfluous or harmful. Similarly, if domestic stabilization policies in the leading countries are planned in harmony with each other, strains on the international monetary and financial system will be manageable. This leaves to the managers of the international monetary system mainly the big problems of speculative and erratic capital movements, which have to be kept under reasonable control. International trade and investment might then be left largely to market forces. Nevertheless, international planning will be necessary to cope with problems of energy supplies, environmental pollution, and food reserves because these cannot be resolved by markets alone.

If the judgment just expressed is correct, the world's new major planning problem is the conscious harmonization of the stabilization policies of leading nations. One institution, the Organization for Economic Cooperation and Development (OECD), already exists as a forum and a source of research for industrial countries. Political leaders have already had summit meetings on such common economic problems as adjustment of exchange rates, pursuit of better-coordinated national policies for inflations and recessions, securing a greater liberalization of international trade, and providing assistance to developing countries who lack the means to pay the high prices of imported oil.

In the United Nations Conference on Trade and Development (UNCTAD) and in special sessions of the United Nations, the developing countries have presented demands for reform of the international economic system and for control of multinational corporations. In long-established institutions such as the World Bank, the International Development Association, various other special-ized agencies, and regional groupings of the United Nations, plans and programs have been developed respecting food and agriculture, environment, regional development, energy, and other pressing problems.

At least one international agency long antedates the numerous other inter-national planning institutions: the General Agreement on Tariffs and Trade

(GATT), set up in the mid-1930s to negotiate agreements to liberalize trade by reducing tariffs and other trade restrictions. The great expansion of international trade and transnational companies is a tribute to the effectiveness of GATT over a period of nearly 50 years. No elaborate planning system or organization produced these results; they were the consequence of a series of agreements negotiated in the common pursuit of the goal of liberalizing international trade.

The above examples of international cooperation serve only to emphasize that the United States is deeply involved in international economic planning. The direction of international planning activities in the United States, however, differs from that of most other advanced countries in that it is fragmented and disorganized, often reflecting more the conflict of domestic interests than international needs. It has often been said of U.S. international negotiations that the most important of them is negotiation among agencies of the U.S. government to determine what our position will be. We engage in cooperative international planning without the benefit or guidance of a coherent plan at home that is consistent with it.

THE CONFUSING ROLE OF BUSINESS IN INTERNATIONAL ECONOMIC PLANNING

What is the role of business leadership in international economic planning? As measured by the CED's efforts, it was in the forefront and on the winning side in its support of measures to restore the international monetary system, to reconstruct international trade and investment, and to rebuild the postwar economies of Europe and Japan. But even in these famous efforts, and in their subsequent extension and modification, business spoke with many voices. A large proportion of the business community supported the unconscionable Smoot-Hawley tariff (1930), was divided on the original Trade Agreements Act (1934), and has only gradually reduced its opposition in the several renewals of that act. It was divided on the Bretton Woods proposals and later on the reform of the international monetary system. The voice of business has not been important in the establishing of new international agencies, although normal business activity has spawned a large number of transnational corporations and an enormous expansion of international trade and investment.

There are two main reasons for this history of neglect by business of international economic developments, aside from selfish private interest. First is the tradition that government is responsible for international relations, and government has not sought the advice of any broad representation of business on most international issues. Second is that until recent times the international market has been of minor importance to U.S. business, accounting for a mere 4 to 5 percent of the U.S. GNP. Under these circumstances, most of U.S. business was not much concerned about the international economy in peacetime.

But now international trade accounts for almost 10 percent of our GNP and is responsible, directly or indirectly, for one out of every seven U.S. jobs.

It is estimated that companies responsible for 60 percent of industrial value added in the United States consider themselves to have substantial interests in production abroad. Domestic and international production and marketing are integrated as never before. What is not integrated in a meaningful way is the knowledge of the private sector with that of government in the making of public and private international economic policies.

Permanent civil servants and duly appointed advisers from the worlds of business, science, and other relevant sectors seldom sit down, agree on problems and the goals to be sought, and seek by discussion and study to find workable means of getting from here to there. The contrast between U.S. and foreign practice in making international economic policy and integrating private and public knowledge and resources is illustrated by some reflections derived from participating in international conferences.

At one of many weekend conferences held in an eighteenth century country house in England, the highest-ranking U.K. minister opened the discussion by expressing his appreciation for information shared by industry with his government on such matters as planned expansion of capacity and new marketing areas at home and, as he added quietly, abroad. Present were heads of industry from Common Market countries, Japan, and the United States. The fact that the minister could speak openly about sharing information on not only his own country's industrial plans but also the plans of competitors in the Common Market and Japan exhibited a closeness of relations between government and business, which, to this writer, was not surprising but which had implications that, upon reflection, were intellectually jolting.

The discussion covered in some detail the sources of information on advance plans for heavy investment industries producing steel, paper, aluminum, chemicals, and other materials sold not only at home but worldwide. One participant admitted that sometimes it was necessary to use industrial espionage to obtain the requisite information about competitors' plans. As the United Kingdom's industry had been lagging in expansion and exports, the topic was of vital concern to the U.K. government representatives who were present. Their objective was to have U.K.-based industry catch up with the parade, and the government was eager to find out how it could best be of assistance to industrial expansion projects and, of course, how industry could be of assistance to government in formulating plans for expansion.

The intellectual jolt to the author was a little slow in coming because so many pieces from so many conferences had to fall together to reveal the significance of what was going on in that friendly, open discussion. At its conclusion the most significant impression was derived not from what was said but from what was not said. The fact that U.S. industrial executives present said not a word bespoke volumes: anything they might have said during a discussion dealing with expansion of capacity and market penetration could have become grounds for prosecution under the U.S. antitrust laws affecting their companies. This inhibition to meaningful participation in government decision making at home and abroad is one of the deep-seated reasons for opposition to national planning by U.S. business leaders.

While virtually all industrial countries have some kind of legislation covering anticompetitive practice, they also have significant provision for what might be called benign cartels. In some countries large industries are either government owned or government financed; the close relationship between government and business ensures the former, at least, that cartel activities will be in keeping with national economic goals and plans. The British share with the Common Market countries provisions in the Treaty of Rome that provide for benign cartels that further the purposes of the Common Market and participating countries and that call for registration of such cartels with the Common Market Commission as a symbol of their legitimacy (and insurance against lawsuits).

Governments of Common Market countries, the Common Market Commission, and the Japanese government, far from wishing to break up large industries or even cartels, prefer to use them to further their own national purposes. (In 1977 the Common Market and Japanese steel interests, according to press reports and U.S. industry allegations, agreed to a limitation on Japanese steel exports to Europe; this intensified Japanese steel exports to the United States. The U.S. steel industry called for and received protection from imports of foreign steel.)

The Japanese government had earlier fostered the merger of the nation's steel companies until in the name of Nippon Steel it had put together the biggest steel company in the world. The British adopted a different tactic in nationalizing and consolidating what is now government-owned British Steel, whose continuing large losses must be made up by government. Preceding organization of the Common Market, member companies established the European Coal and Steel Community to bring about a consolidation and a common policy, which has made the European steel industry far more competitive than it might otherwise have been. On a lesser scale in these same countries, similar acts and policies for coordination and consolidation in other industries have occurred. Let it be noted that there were no ideological commitments to laissez-faire to inhibit such actions.

The United States has unwittingly encouraged cooperation among foreign industries through its handling of international trade incursions into the U.S. market. It requests the country from which the export trade incursion emanates to establish voluntary controls on exports to the United States, thus necessitating a high degree of cooperation among foreign producers and between them and their governments. It is not surprising that so-called voluntary export quotas have been used before for steel and other products by Japan and the Common Market countries. They have also been used recently to limit the export to the United States of color television sets by Japan and shoes by Taiwan and South Korea. There are dozens of voluntary foreign export quotas designed to mitigate the degree of penetration into the U.S. market by producers in other industrial countries. Comparable action by the United States would be virtually impossible. We would put business executives in jail before we would allow them to cooperate to the extent we insist that their foreign competitors do.

The extent to which governments and businesses cooperate abroad for the purpose of penetrating world markets may help to explain why the United States accounted for only 25 percent of the world's production in 1976, whereas 20 years before its share had been about 40 percent. Much of the gain by foreign producers represents the success of our previous foreign economic policy, but further gains may signal an erosion of U.S. productivity, a subject that is central to a later chapter.

Clearly, U.S. policy and planning of foreign trade must be improved to cope with the growing demand for orderly market agreements already in use to control imports of textiles and likely to be negotiated for a broad range of other imported products. We have yet to cope effectively with tariff preferences to the products of developing countries. The French have already resolved the semantic riddle; they are calling for organized free trade – planning.

The problem of declining U.S. productivity, however, runs much deeper than that of meeting foreign competition in international trade. Leading competitor nations have adopted industrial policies, the use of government aid and disincentives to shift the production mix toward higher productivity lines and to phase out declining industries – a rudimentary form of national planning. Only a part of this industrial policy has been introduced in the United States: the rescue and support of declining industries – not picking the winners but the losers.

The incompatibility of U.S. domestic institutions, practices, and philosophies with those of foreign countries is understood by relatively few business leaders. Some of our most important planning problems in coming years will stem from this incompatibility.

CAN NATIONAL PLANNING BE FOR PEOPLE?

Up to this point, I have expressed the views of makers of economic policy – views that fall somewhere between those of economists and business leaders. There is a wealth of literature and knowledge on economic aspects of planning, but national planning is for people, who have so far been identified only as actors in the arena: the economy. We know very little about how people's quality of life might be improved by systemwide planning. After all, in the so-called industrial democracies government and business are supposed to operate for the benefit of the people, not of government bureaucrats and politicians, or business executives and employees, or academicians. For planning to be more than an intellectual game or an ad hoc rescue of losers, it must be directed toward improving the quality of life of those who constitute the society, not simply as economic persons who work, save, and spend but as sentient, thinking, aspiring human beings, young and old, male and female in all their individual personalities. To mention this ultimate goal of planning is to open a Pandora's box of unknown dimensions and complexity, because the behavioral sciences are only beginning to discover the relationships between social and economic policies and their effects on real, individual human beings.

What do people consider important to their quality of life, and how well satisfied are they with it? Pioneer research by John Flanagan and his associates at the American Institutes for Research provides some interesting insights into what the guidelines of planning might be.[4] As social psychologists, Flanagan and associates asked nationwide cross sections of 30-, 50-, and 70-year-olds what were important aspects of their quality of life, how important to it were the components they identified, and how well their needs for each component were being met.

On "importance to quality of life," the economists' prototype of economic man did not turn up at the top, nor were most of the valued qualities of life even in the economists' ball park.

The highest-ranking component for any life quality was "health and personal safety." This component was rated as being important or very important to the respondent's quality of life by 95 to 98 percent of males and females in all three age groups. But only between 80 and 86 percent reported that their needs in this category were being well met — a disparity between the high rating of *importance* and the lesser rating of *satisfaction*, which ranged between 10 and 17 percent for the six groups.

There is little in the preceding discussion of planning that is related to providing remedies for deficiency in this most important self-identified component in the quality of people's lives. Health care and personal safety are in the province of self-service or local delivery systems of widely varying quality. The subjects are not high on the agenda of the federal government, which at present has little capacity to deliver anything but money to support these highest-rated life qualities.

"Interesting, rewarding worthwhile work" was the next-highest ranking component of quality of life for 30- and 50-year-olds of both sexes. Work was ranked high in importance by 89 percent of these people, with 78 percent reporting their needs well or very well met. (Being mostly retired, 70-year-olds were subtracted, but 55 percent of the men and 59 percent of the women in this group still rated work as important, and 75 percent or more reported their needs well met.)

"Having and raising children" ranked third in importance with an average rating of more than 87 percent. Needs well met was reported by 83 percent, with women expressing a higher proportion of needs well met than men.

The component having the fourth-highest average ranking in importance — so rated by an average of almost 83 percent of the male groups and 90 percent of the female groups — will further surprise economists and planners. It is "understanding yourself." Of the men an average of 75 percent report needs well met compared with 76 percent of the women, who in general gave this component much higher importance than did the men.

Fifth ranking in importance, with an average of 83 percent, was the object of the economist's affection: "material comforts" — home, income security, and the like. Almost 75 percent of the respondents considered that their needs were well met, a finding that casts some doubt on the economist's axiom that wants are insatiable.

Sixth ranking as to importance to quality of life, with an average of 81 percent for all groups, was a "close relationship with spouse or person of the opposite sex." For male groups the average was 88 percent; for female groups, 74 percent. (The lower average for women is the result of a 46 percent importance rating by 70-year-olds, half of whom are widows.) The average percentage of all groups reporting needs well met is only two percentage points lower than that for importance. (Far more 70-year-old women report needs well met — 70 percent — than report the relationship important — 46 percent.)

The leading examples just recited of the findings from in-depth personal interviews of representative individuals from all walks of life — male and female and 30, 50, and 70 years of age — provide some insight into the problems involved in national planning for a nation of people as diverse as ours. I have cited only a few of the findings but hopefully enough to demonstrate that if planning is for people, we need to know a great deal more than we now do about what they value and what they feel they need but have not realized.

Still another lesson is to be derived from these studies. Who was interested in learning what quality-of-life surveys might tell us? Business? So far as I know, business has supported few, if any, of the pioneer studies. Government? Only after certain nonprofit research groups had staked their own modest reserves on pilot studies did government agencies evidence interest, and then only after studies were restructured to reflect the agencies' narrow orientation toward such research. Advocates of national planning? Without any reference to this kind of research, the Initiative Committee for National Planning sponsored the drafting of the Humphrey-Javits bill.

It is probably safe to conclude that most members of the planning movement in the United States wish to reflect their own values from the top down and that opponents of it share the same myopia.

The door is open and the way unobstructed for those who genuinely desire a society and a government that reflect the values of the people that constitute the foundation of their concern. Planning in the United States will make sound progress when it is identified with the sources of its strength and impetus: the values and aspirations of people who are the beneficiaries or victims of any plans that are made. Until we can be sure that national planning can be founded on this basis, we would be well advised to stay with what we now have — planning for stable growth of the economy.

The fiscal-monetary-international planning that was described earlier is for limited objectives: levels of employment and real income in the closest approximation to a market system that we can achieve. This type of planning takes pride in being impersonal, not concerned with individual quality of life, and directed only toward the bread-and-butter necessities, which, when provided, allow freedom for people to choose their own life-styles — so long as they do not interfere with the functioning of the economic system.

From a quality-of-life point of view, the economy is inefficient; witness the high importance of health and safety compared with the rating of how well needs are met. It is inefficient in the organization and supply of government services for health care and safety largely because government does not apply the logic and processes of private sector delivery, namely, finding what is wanted and providing it with efficiency. Nevertheless, buttressed by income security in the form of Social Security, unemployment insurance, and welfare and by the policing of abuses to environment, product quality, safety, and monopoly power, it does deliver goods and services well enough to cause almost 75 percent of the population surveyed to rate their need for material comfort well met.

Improvement of that rating is a challenging objective that could probably be attained without a major restructuring of either the economy or the society. And it is an objective that must begin with careful identification of individual needs, not general-purpose infusions of purchasing power that are expected to trickle down to the neediest. Here, indeed, is one of the great gaps in social science research. It is a research gap that could be closed by additions or, better, by substitutions in the budgets of government and business that would not be noticed.

NOTES

1. Frederick J. Turner, *The Frontier in American History* (Huntington, N.Y.: Krieger, 1976).

2. Solomon Fabricant, "The Growth of the American Economy, 1776-2001," in *Business and the American Economy*, ed. Jules Backman (New York: New York University Press, 1976).

3. Testimony on Murray bill, 1945, from Karl Schriftgiesser, *Business Comes of Age* (New York: Harper, 1960), p. 97.

4. The findings summarized here are mainly from John Flanagan and Darlene Russ-Eft, "Identifying Opportunities for Improving the Quality of Life of Older Age Groups," Program Report for the Administration on Aging. Mimeographed. Washington, D.C.: Department of Health, Education and Welfare, September 1977.

3

THE CONTINUING SEARCH FOR HIGH EMPLOYMENT WITHOUT INFLATION

The imaginative economist-business executive Beardsley Ruml, one of the country's effective policy shapers for many years, became solicitous about my education soon after we met in policy-making work in the 1950s. The first time it was convenient, he buttonholed me to impart the magic formula for turning opinionated top executives into apostles dedicated to government fiscal intervention to attain a high-employment economy and keep it that way. His educational campaign had a continued impact; the successful 1980 Republican candidate for president, and his platform, advocated large across-the-board tax cuts to stimulate the economy.

"Business people," said Ruml, "will almost without exception agree with two principles. The first is that we ought to have a balanced [federal] budget. The second is that the country ought to have high employment. Put those two principles together and you get the 'stabilizing budget': a balanced budget at high employment."[1] He beamed and added that this argument eventually swung business executive support behind the Employment Act of 1946 and toleration of deficits that occurred when unemployment increased above an acceptable level — at the time, and not for very good reasons, about 3 to 4 percent. The rule first promulgated in a 1947 CED policy statement continued virtually unchanged until it was refined in 1968, but it is still a basic part of the country's budget policy. A recent statement of it is included in Figure 1.

The "fiscalist" program for economic stabilization grew out of the necessities of fighting depression and was accompanied by a virtual revolution in economic thinking. Academics who in the 1930s had to turn to economists such as John Hobson and Foster and Catchings in their search for understanding the Great Depression (1929-33) had gained quick wisdom from J. M. Keynes's *General Theory* (1936).[2] Most of my generation of college students

FIGURE 1
The Stabilizing Budget Policy

The main principles of a stabilizing (federal) budget policy can be summarized as follows:

> The impact of the budget should vary with the condition of the economy as a whole, being more expansive when the economy is depressed and more restrictive when the economy is booming or inflationary.

> The overall impact that the budget exerts upon the economy should not, when combined with appropriate monetary and other policies, be so restrictive that it makes attainment of high employment ordinarily unlikely or so expansive that it leads to persistent inflation.

To achieve these objectives, the federal government should normally set its expenditure programs and tax rates at levels that would yield a moderate budget surplus on a national income and product account basis under conditions of high employment and price stability.

The high-employment budget position should permit an adequate flow of funds to the private credit markets and to the markets for state and local securities, should not call for excessive tightness of monetary policy, and should help to promote sound economic growth.

Variations in tax yields, which rise and fall proportionately more than national income, and changes in government expenditures for unemployment assistance and other programs when unemployment changes tend to cushion variations in total personal income and thereby lessen fluctuations in demand.

If demand conditions deviate significantly from those on which the stabilizing budget is based, flexible adjustments in a stabilizing direction should be made in income tax rates.

Source: Committee for Economic Development, *Fighting Inflation and Promoting Growth* (New York: CED, 1976).

had to search the unfavored authors or wait for this new enlightenment, which enjoyed immediate respectability in academic circles. When, before the new enlightenment, I joined with a group of earnest seniors in a petition to our university's economics department to provide lectures or seminars about the depression of the 1930s then paralyzing the country, the honest reply that we received from the department was, "We do not know enough to be able to comply with your request." In this day of instant analysis for news media, the state of knowledge may be the same, but there is no lack of presumptuous pundits to supply answers off the shelf.

By 1947, a little more than a decade after Keynes's *General Theory* was published, mature Republican business executives could get a serviceable diagnosis and prescription from the stabilizing budget principle and a good short course in how to deal with business cycles from a 75-page policy statement entitled *Taxes and the Budget*, published by the CED in 1947.[3] Its argument was not based on mathematical demonstration but on an appeal to the common sense of business executives after carefully taking account of their prejudices.

The stabilizing budget principle contained much more than met the eye. Because the government's budget could be calculated with revenues and expenditures in balance at high employment, the rule called simply for allowing government deficits to occur when the economy went into recession and unemployment increased. The decline in tax revenues and the increase in unemployment compensation, together with farm price-support payments and the increase in welfare expenditures, were enough to ensure that such deficits occurred. Government borrowing to cover the government deficits offset repayment of loans by businesses and others as they experienced reduced sales and unloaded inventories. Increased payments by government to the unemployed, the poor, and farmers helped to maintain personal incomes. The vicious spiral of declining incomes and contracting credit, which characterized the Great Depression of the 1930s (and most other recessions), could be avoided.

Much importance was attached by business executives who originated the stabilizing budget policy to the fact that it could be applied without relying on forecasts that were and still are liable to large errors in crucial times, including the recessions of 1974/75 and the one beginning in 1980 but forecast for 1979 by most economists. All that was needed was not a forecast but a calculation of the high-employment values of the government's receipts and expenditures. Table 1 illustrates this concept.

The stabilizing budget called for the same calculation of a high-employment budget in surplus when the economy was overexpanding and inflationary price increases were occurring. Under these conditions, the progressive income tax on individuals pushed countless people into higher tax brackets and so increased tax receipts at a faster rate than incomes, a quick-action response because of tax withholding (another Ruml invention called the pay-as-you-go plan, introduced at the beginning of World War II). Inflationary conditions also increase nominal corporate profits and taxes, a subject treated at length in the next

TABLE 1
Actual and High-Employment Federal Receipts and Expenditures,
National Income and Product Accounts, Calendar Years 1973-80
(in billions of dollars)

Calendar Year or Quarter	Actual				High-Employment[a]			
			Surplus or Deficit (−)				Surplus or Deficit (−)	
	Receipts	Expenditures	Amount	Percent of GNP	Receipts	Expenditures	Amount	Percent of GNP[b]
1973	258.6	264.2	−5.6	−0.4	252.7	264.0	−11.3	−0.9
1974	287.8	299.3	−11.5	−.8	296.9	297.6	−.7	−.1
1975	287.3	356.6	−69.3	−4.5	315.8	344.9	−29.1	−2.2
1976	331.8	384.8	−53.1	−3.1	354.7	374.8	−20.1	−1.5
1977	375.1	421.5	−46.4	−2.4	390.7	413.8	−23.1	−1.6
1978	431.5	460.7	−29.2	−1.4	441.1	456.8	−15.7	−1.1
1979	494.4	509.2	−14.8	−.6	504.2	506.5	−2.2	−.1
1980[c]	538.9	601.2	−62.3	−2.4	573.2	591.6	−18.3	−1.2

[a]These totals differ from those published in the November 1980 *Survey of Current Business* because of revisions to both actual and potential GNP.
[b]High-employment surplus or deficit as percentage of high-employment GNP.
[c]Preliminary.

Note: Detail may not add to totals because of rounding.

Source: U.S., Department of Commerce (Bureau of Economic Analysis), Office of Management and Budget, and Council of Economic Advisers, *Economic Report of the President* (Washington, D.C.: Government Printing Office, January 1981), p. 157.

39

chapter. Tax revenues increase automatically in an economy undergoing inflation and can generate a government budget surplus while at the same time
leaving both business and consumers with nominal incomes unchanged or
increased. The government surplus permits repayment of government debt
held by banks and others and enables banks, if they are so disposed, to increase
loans to private sector borrowers without adding to the money supply.

What if — perhaps as the result of a violation of the stabilizing budget rule —
there is a recession or an inflationary boom? Then the stabilizing budget policy
calls for an increase in the dosage that the stabilization rule suggests. The
quickest way is by an across-the-board tax cut if the economy needs stimulation and an across-the-board tax increase if the need is to curb an excess of
aggregate demand. Slower, more primitive, and, therefore, less effective ways
of stimulating the economy were to increase public works projects and public
sector jobs (for example, the Comprehensive Employment and Training Act
[CETA] program). Both methods have returned to prominence but without
overcoming the defects demonstrated in earlier experience: very long time
lags in public works programs and considerable waste in emergency jobs
programs. Unfortunately, the rule does not cover conditions when both recession and inflation occur simultaneously — conditions that occur infrequently but
that dominated the 1970s and extended into the 1980s. Much of this book is
devoted to an analysis and treatment for that new dilemma of policy makers.

The stabilizing budget had built into it some surprisingly ingenious means of
carrying out a philosophy of fiscal policy strongly espoused by business executives. That philosophy was to reduce the role of government in the economy
and, especially, to reduce the tax burden. This has helped to account for the
stabilizing budget's longevity despite its undermining by many economists and
politicians who did not like its spartan implications. For example, as the
economy grew and tax revenues increased, unless new government-spending
programs were started or old ones enlarged, there would be a growing surplus
as a high level of employment occurred. The surplus would allow taxes to be
cut. Executives and their political friends used such opportunities on several
occasions to argue strongly and with some success for permanent tax reductions, especially of corporate taxes and high-bracket income taxes. More
recently, the CED in its policy statement *Fighting Inflation and Promoting
Growth* modified the rule to call for a substantial surplus at high employment
(instead of balance) to provide funds for reducing the government debt in order
to return capital needed by the private sector for investment in new plants and
equipment, a subject considered more fully in the next chapter.[4]

CONGRESS AND THE STABILIZING BUDGET

While there were conceptual inadequacies in the stabilizing budget policy
that I will discuss later, one of the serious shortcomings was that it did not fit

the political process in effect during most of the period from its inception until recently. Congress had to act not only on the regular budget but on any emergency tax cut or tax increase that the rule called for. In the budget-making process until 1975, even Congress itself did not know how big the budget would be until more than a year after the budget was proposed. How, then, could it act on a tax cut (or increase) quickly? Moreover, the House, and especially the Ways and Means Committee, which has jurisdiction over tax bills, insisted on preserving its prerogatives. We were advised repeatedly by chairmen of the Ways and Means Committee that shortcuts to give the president limited power to raise or lower income taxes, even within rigid limits, would not be enacted — economists and business people to the contrary notwithstanding. A stabilizing tax bill had to be acted on quickly to be effective, and policy discussions of executives and economists for many years were prolonged by unsuccessful attempts to devise a method to give the president authority to promulgate a temporary tax change that would take effect without going through the long congressional tax-writing process.

After economists and business executives had failed for a quarter of a century to devise a way to cut or raise taxes expeditiously for stabilization purposes, it was Congress itself, aided by another CED committee (Improving Management in Government), that came at the problem from another direction, which proved ultimately to provide the key.[5] The winning approach was to address the congressional budget-making process itself in terms of the needs of the economy.

Congress, to the amazement of most, reorganized its processes in the Budget and Impoundment Act of 1974, more than a quarter of a century after the need was recognized for an expeditious way to raise or cut taxes for stabilization purposes. The presence of *impoundment* in the title indicates that Nixon administration impoundments of appropriated funds at least accelerated the process of congressional reform of budget making. Under the new procedures the president proposes and Congress early in the year acts upon the budget as a whole, a budget that is geared to the need for fiscal action to stabilize the economy. The new system has been tested; it performed well in achieving a quick tax cut in 1977, although not of the simple across-the-board variety. It was to be tested again in 1981.

EMERGENCIES AND FISCAL STABILIZATION

Not foreseen by the progenitors of the stabilizing budget policy were the number of occasions when stabilizing tax changes of an emergency nature (for example, going beyond the limits of the rule) would be called for. The outbreak of the Korean War was an early instance. A small group of seasoned trustee executives in the CED authorized to apply existing policy recommendations to current conditions immediately issued a statement calling for a tax increase and other fiscal measures and followed up with a policy statement in 1951 calling for an increase in taxes of $10 billion, an amount later recommended by President Harry S. Truman but reduced by Congress to $5.7 billion. This increase, together with the added tax revenue generated by a fast-growing economy, made the Korean War financing a model of fiscal conservatism compared with the Vietnam episode. While price and wage controls were imposed for a time in the Korean War, fiscal policy soon made them redundant.

The most difficult problem for policy makers is always that of having enough information. To propose drastic fiscal policy changes without any essential information is either to have vision, to be brave, or to be foolish. Toward the end of 1966, business leaders were faced with this choice. The Vietnam War effort was being stepped up, and there were many signs that the economy was becoming overheated. Yet the most vital facts about what was going on were missing. The usual midyear federal budget review had been omitted; the state of the budget, aside from some overall income and expenditure figures, had last been reported nearly a year earlier. At a meeting in the fall of 1966, a concerned group of executives heard reports based on personal sources of information that only the secretary of defense and the president knew what was in the defense budget and its current status; the director of the budget did not. The Federal Reserve was equally unaware of the current state of the budget and was obviously handicapped (during those days before money aggregates were considered a sufficient guide) in conducting monetary policy. (We learned only later that the secretary of the treasury and the chairman of the Council of Economic Advisers had earlier recommended a tax increase to the president, who had replied that he would not propose a tax increase because Congress would not consider it. He also told these advisers not to engage in public discussion of the matter – in effect, to say nothing.)

Several among the group of executives anxiously considering the problem had information on orders and shipments of war materials and supplies that they did not disclose but that helped them to form educated judgments. The role of such undisclosed information in private policy-making groups is usually underrated.

After prayerful consideration, the small group of executives made its decision: it would recommend an emergency tax increase in keeping with the principle of the stabilizing fiscal policy. While students rioted in the colleges and the streets, the executives in the CED at least read the fiscal riot act to the country's political leaders. The key paragraphs of the statement follow.

Without inflation, the normal growth of the economy would increase the annual yield of the existing tax system by about $6 or $7 billion from one year to the next. But this is far below the recent rate of increase of expenditures. From the third quarter of 1965 to the third quarter of 1966, federal expenditures increased by $18.8 billion, of which $10.6 billion was for national defense and $8.2 billion for other purposes.

It is perfectly clear now that much of the surplus in the first half of 1966 came from inflation, which raised personal incomes, profits and, consequently, tax revenues. We paid the unfair and insidious tax of inflation rather than taxing ourselves openly and fairly. The inflation that has happened has happened, and probably cannot be undone except at great pain. But we must now plan to attain a surplus that will avoid more inflation.

We recommend, therefore, that expenditure and tax decisions should be made by the new Congress early next year that would yield a surplus in excess of $3 billion at high employment and the price level now prevailing. This surplus should be provided by reduction in government expenditures, but to the extent that sufficient expenditure reduction is not achieved the surplus must be provided by an increase in revenues. Such additional revenues should be raised by an across-the-board increase in taxes limited to one year.[6]

The statement carrying this recommendation was issued in December 1966. The president called for a tax increase in the spring of 1967. Consideration of it by Congress began in the fall, and it was finally enacted in the summer of 1968. Meanwhile, from a near balance in the budget in 1965 and 1966, in 1967 the deficit increased to more than $14 billion. Wholesale prices, which had been relatively stable for ten years preceding 1965, began a sharp increase that mounted to 12.5 percent above the 1965 level by 1969 and attained a momentum that continued upward in the following years. Had the advice to increase taxes, given in 1966, been followed promptly, the endemic inflation that began then might have been either avoided or very much moderated.

Other occasions for ad hoc stabilizing tax changes were happier, calling for tax reductions rather than increases. A tax cut in 1964, recommended by President John Kennedy in 1961 and the CED in 1962, was probably the first general tax reduction taken explicitly to stimulate the economy. Its success apparently influenced President Ronald Reagan's campaign in 1980. Action was taken in 1964 so long after it was needed that the stabilizing value of the cut was dubious. The CED also recommended a stimulating tax reduction at the end of 1976. This cut, made in early 1977, was the first to be accomplished expeditiously, thanks to reform of the congressional budgetary process referred to earlier.

From time to time the question was raised whether adherence to a stabilizing budget policy would have resulted in a more stable economy at a high level than the policies actually followed — for example, a long delay before the tax cut of 1964 and the increase of 1968; and inaction in the recessions of 1953/54 and 1957/58. Econometric studies simulating application of a high-employment budget rule have shown that the economy would have been more stable at better levels than were achieved by the tardy policies actually followed.

THE HIGH-EMPLOYMENT BUDGET

The high-employment budget calculation has become a regular exercise in the President's Economic Report. This budget shows the surplus or deficit in the budget as it would be if the economy were moving at high employment along its potential growth path. It does not reflect the changes in actual receipts and expenditures resulting from cyclical fluctuations in the economy. Therefore, it indicates whether the fiscal policy actually embodied in the budget would be expansive or contractive at a high-employment level. A high-employment deficit would be expansionary; a high-employment surplus would be restrictive. Table 1 shows actual and high-employment budgets for 1973 through 1980. Note that the actual budget for 1979 was in deficit but that the high-employment budget was in surplus and therefore exercised a small restrictive effect, probably much too small in retrospect. None of the high-employment deficits or surpluses in the 1970s were large enough to represent a vigorous fiscal policy; note their small percentage of GNP. The stabilizing budget policy is firmly embedded in the making of fiscal policy. While it is probably insufficient for maintaining full employment under all circumstances, it is widely agreed that it is a most important element in an effective government stabilization policy.

To this point, the problem of stabilization has been considered only in terms of fiscal policy. The framers of the stabilizing budget policy did not neglect monetary policy but gave it a relatively minor role of being accommodative to an appropriate fiscal policy. In 1968, 20 years after the stabilizing budget concept was recommended, a subcommittee considered the question of why monetary policy had earlier been assigned a limited role. Some argued that it was because the major job had been given to fiscal policy, which was specifically measurable, and that the strong role of fiscal policy could be tolerated only because monetary policy could be used to correct mistakes or, as one executive put it, could be used as a safeguard against a "gutless" fiscal policy. The reasoning behind the assignment of a limited role to monetary policy is supported by the facts about the misuse of monetary policy in the early postwar years. The Federal Reserve in the postwar period was until 1951 a prisoner of its own policy of pegging the prices of government securities during and after World War II. No group of informed people in the postwar period before 1951 would have assigned any large stabilizing role to such a one-way monetary policy, and distrust continued for a long time. Executives in the CED leaned toward heavy reliance upon a policy instrument that could move in either direction — toward contraction or expansion. Many also argued that policies that could produce a recession should be determined by a politically responsible body: Congress.[7]

TOWARD A NEW MIX IN STABILIZATION POLICIES

After a long period of warm relations and interchange between business leaders and the Federal Reserve, the intellectual relationship soured in the first half of the 1970s. CED trustees who had served on the boards of regional Federal Reserve banks and understood Federal Reserve policy well were among the most disenchanted. What brought about the disenchantment was the erratic course of Federal Reserve policy in the first half of the 1970s — not so much the mistakenly easy money policy of 1971/72 as the nearly disastrous tight money policy of 1973/74, pursued into a deep recession at a time of double-digit inflation and double-digit unemployment.

One trustee executive in the equipment industry spoke for most of his colleagues when he argued that time after time the adopted cure for inflation has been to slow down the rate of money supply growth, which raises interest rates, slows the economy, and increases unemployment. He said that we will never control inflation by creating a recession because we cannot tolerate the unemployment that comes with a recession. The politicians will spend government money to put people back to work as they very well should. So what is the answer? He argued that if inflation is the product of too much money in relation to goods, then a better answer is to produce more and invest more to increase the supply of goods, an alternative not given high priority by government. These are views that were widely shared by his colleagues. They will be explored further in the next chapter.

The tightening of monetary policy and a perverse fiscal policy were considered severely damaging to the economy by the trustee executives in the fall of 1974. After a meeting devoted to a discussion of the sad state of the economy, a committee insisted that its voice be raised in protest and with advice about how to overcome double-digit rates of unemployment and inflation. Under the rules of the committee it would have to base its position on a policy statement. The one in process was not ready, and no prior statement came even close to addressing the precarious state into which the economy had fallen. The most expeditious procedure was to commission an official public address on the situation and give it wide circulation.

Philip M. Klutznick, then chairman of the Research and Policy Committee (later secretary of commerce in the Carter administration) accepted the charge. In an address in New York on January 9, 1975 — and before President Gerald Ford delivered his State of the Union and other messages — he made one of the most incisive characterizations of the failures of stabilization policy that had come, even unofficially, from the committee or any other group of executives. I quote at some length from this address because it represents how the body of knowledge developed within the CED, with help from economic advisers, over a period of nearly 30 years could be applied under conditions bordering on an economic crisis. Because influential people in business, government, and the media had in one way or another been educated in that body of knowledge, the address had a very large impact. It is excerpted here with the permission of the author.

To be complacent and ignore the danger signals is to refuse to recognize a phenomenon unknown in peacetime history. Price rises brought us in November [1974] to the largest twelve-month increase [in prices] since September 1947 — a whopping 12.6 percent! At the same time, production fell, and the rate of unemployment . . . reached the highest level in fourteen years. Recession shares with inflation the dubious role of public enemy number one.

. . . Meanwhile, back at the controls, the engineers have been running the engines of stabilization in reverse: in a period of recession they have *reduced* the *real money supply* while pursuing an increasingly *restrictive* fiscal policy. . . . [When the data became available, it was found that the high-employment budget in 1974, as the recession deepened, was in surplus by nearly $10 billion.]

Along with appropriate money and budget policies, we need a new generation of economic solutions to deal with a young and stubborn generation of economic problems. And these solutions, in my opinion, cannot be effective unless they recognize the major elements in the changing economic landscape.

1.   The discipline of fixed exchange rates is no longer the controlling influence in world monetary affairs. . . . We no longer have to take the medicine of higher unemployment to remedy our balance of payments deficits.

2.   Chronic surpluses of U.S. farm products have been replaced by scarcities and depleted food reserves [because of uncontrolled buying by the Soviet Union].

3.   The era of cheap and abundant energy and raw materials in the United States has ended.

4.   The government has failed to find a means of shortcutting and stopping the insidious game of leap-frog in wages and prices. Business and labor have to share the blame and help together to find the remedy.

5.   Economic policy has become excessively addicted to manipulation of the money supply as the principal instrument of economic stabilization. In 1972 and '73, when we needed fiscal and monetary restraint, the high-employment budget, corrected for inflation, . . . ran large annual deficits and we poured money into the economy as if it were going out of style. . . . Our commercial banking system has been operating like yo-yos with interest rates climbing up at a dizzy pace and then beginning the inevitable slide down. At best, monetary policy is both inequitable and inadequate as a stabilization instrument.

I believe that considerable easing of monetary pressure is desirable as part of an overall program to turn the economy around. My concern with loosening the money supply is with the past failure to take steps to redress the misallocation of that money to the detriment of the economy. Available credits should not be used to feed the inflation. There is growing evidence that, at current rates of interest, funds placed to the credit of certain businesses result in passing on increased interest costs in the form of increased prices. An urgent aspect of any easing of monetary restrictions is the need to direct the use of available funds into areas of greatest distress. . . .

The myth that we do not want to complicate our procedures by credit allocation defeats itself by the obvious fact that allocation is taking place by default. And in many instances the defaults are damaging to inflation control.

A lender of last resort to the private sector must be established to handle individual liquidity crises — and especially to supply long-term capital for energy investments and investments that will relieve supply bottlenecks. Most of this can be done by guarantees. And . . . federal agencies should devise incentives to encourage the use of variable interest-rate home mortgages. [Action was subsequently taken to implement both proposals.]

Fiscal policy should, as CED's stabilizing budget rule requires, turn decisely toward the expansive side. I believe the size of the fiscal stimulus should be in the order of $25 billion. For comparison, let me remind you that the tax cut of $11 billion in 1964 would be equivalent to $26 billion in today's economy. This much stimulation is needed to stop the downslide in our economy and to start it moving up again. The resulting increase in the government's deficit, moreover, would help to offset the deflationary effect of the forced savings [indirect taxation] of $25 billion or more resulting from higher oil prices. . . .

This Committee has in years past advocated a number of anti-recession measures, but I suggest that they be carefully reviewed to make sure they do not compound future inflation. Extended unemployment compensation and federal welfare payments . . . can minimize the human costs of a recession without excessively aggravating inflation, *providing* these "safety nets" do not become an alibi for prolonged deviations from high employment. If they do, they will only undermine productivity and thus weaken the fight against inflation.

Now I speak of wages and prices. [We have] in the past taken the position (quite unorthodox for a business group at the time) that some continuing direct governmental concern with significant wage and price decisions must play a role in the nation's overall stabilization strategy. I believe that principle continues to make sense. But when the government explores the various means of putting that principle into practice, it runs into all kinds of trouble, particularly when we face the double-trouble of inflation and recession. . . .

The desirability of a tax cut to break the momentum of the wage-price spiral is self-evident. Higher and higher wage settlements are simply not the answer. They merely push prices higher and further erode the real income of wage earners.

To compensate lower and middle income groups for the erosion of their buying power, I support a reduction of taxes on the first $15,000 a year of income sufficient to offset the amount by which real hourly wages seem to have declined in the last year − 3 percent. This would amount to about $20 billion and would require a reduction in personal income tax liabilities of about 15 percent and, of course, much more than that on lower incomes. Such action would release additional purchasing power while reducing pressures for another inflationary bulge in wages. With appropriate restraints this is a weapon well suited for fighting on two fronts: inflation and recession. [The income tax credit to offset the Social Security tax increase proposed by the administration in 1980 was based on the same reasoning.]

Now I want to suggest the kind of restraints to accompany the tax cut which would make it effective in the two-front attack. That suggestion is that the Congress should include in the legislation an explicit declaration of intent that the tax cut is being made as part of a social compact among business, labor, and government to restrain future inflation. For labor, the compact calls for limiting wage increases. . . . If wage increases on average exceed the guidelines, the tax reduction could be progressively reduced and in fact could be framed with such automatic reduction built in. [In effect, this is a proposal for a TIP − tax-based incomes policy.]

If labor and government are expected to produce a "social compact" on wages, business should do no less on prices. . . . But this should be done in exchange for a guarantee that price controls will not be reimposed.

The address received wide attention in the media and was widely circulated in the government. It was followed up by testimony along the same lines by Klutznick before the Ways and Means Committee in late January 1975 and before the Joint Economic Committee in February.

The New York *Times* in a long editorial the day after the speech was delivered endorsed all of its major proposals.[8] President Ford, who as late as the preceding October was calling for a tax increase to fight inflation, on January 15 called for a $15 billion tax cut, largely in the form of income tax rebates for a large and fast effect on incomes. Most media comment preferred the larger figure that Klutznick had recommended.

Congress followed up with a tax cut largely along the lines recommended by the president and later in the year enlarged and extended the reductions into 1976. Tax reductions totaled $10.2 billion in fiscal 1975, $16.7 billion in fiscal 1976, and $18.5 billion in fiscal 1977 − considerable evidence that the stabilizing budget policy was in effect.

THE FAILURE OF RECESSIONS TO STOP INFLATION

Conditions giving rise to the inflation-recession of the 1970s were the series of shocks well described in the policy statements:[9] devaluations of the dollar, which raised important prices and stimulated exports; an overheated economy under price controls, which experienced materials shortages; a quantum jump in oil prices; a huge increase in farm and food prices triggered by purchases of state trading economies without restraint in a U.S. free market; followed by a cyclical recession accentuated by drastic application of a restrictive monetary policy.

Accelerated wage increases stimulated by price inflation and the erosion of real wages, as will be shown, were not dampened by the recession. Food and fuel price increases were not offset by price cutting in other sectors but were, instead, followed by other price increases to pass on higher wage costs. Neither wage nor price increases were prevented or noticeably moderated by an increase in unemployment to double-digit levels. Moreover, similar events occurred in other industrial countries.

The failure of wage increases to become more moderate in recessions is demonstrated in Table 2.

TABLE 2
Average Hourly Compensation in Expansion and Recession, Private Business Sector — All Persons

Cyclical Peak Quarter	Percent Change from Same Quarter of the Preceding Year	Percent Change to Same Quarter of the Following Year	Difference (percentage points)
1948 − IV	8.4	−0.3	−8.8
1953 − II	7.1	3.6	−3.5
1957 − III	6.4	5.3	−1.1
1960 − II	5.2	4.4	−0.8
1969 − IV	6.5	7.0	+0.5
1973 − IV	8.6	10.8	+2.2
1980 − I	8.4	9.8	+1.4*

Source: George Terborgh, *Federal Anti-Inflation Policy*, Mimeographed. (Washington, D.C.: Machinery and Allied Products Institute, 1977.*) Updated by the author.

Whereas in earlier recessions the rates of wage increase slowed down from those in the preceding periods of expansion, in the first year of recession following the cyclical peaks in 1969, 1973, and 1980, the average rate of wage increase actually exceeded that of the last year of each preceding boom. Moreover, in the three years after the cyclical peak in 1973, the average rate of wage increases remained in the prerecession 8 to 10 percent range. Levels of unemployment reached in these recessions were so high that they evoked strong counterrecession government fiscal and public employment policies. Clearly, the country will not stand for a recession-inducing monetary policy strong enough to force much, if any, moderation in wage increases.

Recessions may also tend to prevent rather than stimulate price reductions. This is especially possible in a period of continued inflationary pressure. While such an outcome is considered outrageous if not impossible by many and, perhaps, most economists, there is much convincing testimony and analysis to support it. In those sectors of the economy where investment is high relative to output, and there are relatively few firms, countless executives have argued that when demand falls, there is nothing to be gained and much to be lost by cutting prices in the attempt to maintain sales. Competitors can be expected to match price cuts, especially in a recession. This is especially true for intermediate products and components with a derived demand dependent on sales of big-ticket goods like generators, process equipment, production plants, trucks, and the like. Moreover, because of reduced sales volume, in a recession profits fall and undercosting of depreciation as a result of inflation puts a further obstacle in the way of price cuts because they would reduce cash flow needed to finance new equipment, plants, and inventory. These arguments have been vigorously made by executives in discussions to deride the economists' model-derived expectation of therapeutic price cuts in a recession. (Seldom, however, does anyone mention foreign export pricing in this context; it is obvious that European and Japanese producers use price cutting to maintain or increase export sales in recessions, and much of their exports are to the United States.)

There are other dynamic reasons for maintaining prices that executives do not ignore. There is always the possibility that another set of inflationary shocks will be followed by imposition of price controls. Producers have learned that it is costly to be caught with their prices down. And behind all of these views is the expectation of continuing inflation: Why cut prices when you are certain of upcoming wage increases and other cost increases that will call for raising them? This last view leads to the use of rebates instead of price cuts for durable consumer goods, a common practice in the 1970s and early 1980s.

Producer rationales have been supported by some recent empirical research.[10] Firms with considerable power to set and maintain prices are alleged to govern their prices and volume to achieve a target amount of profit in keeping with that of the past and of similar firms. One way to do this, as well as to measure such behavior, is to apply a factor to direct costs for overhead and profit: a margin. To maintain the target amount of profits when volume falls in a recession, the margin must be increased. To the extent that this can be done, recessions become inflationary because volume reductions must be followed by increased markups that are usually achieved by higher prices or prices that are maintained when costs fall or reduced quality and service, more extras, and so forth.

This hypothesis was tested for five recent recessions beginning with that of 1948/49 on industries classified as high concentration (more than 50 percent of output by the largest four producers), low concentration (less than 25 percent produced by the largest four), and medium concentration (15 to 50 percent produced by the largest four).

With the exception of the 1969/70 recession in which differences among the three groups were insignificant, the remaining four recessions showed an increase in average markup for the high-concentration industries, whereas the low- and medium-concentration industries sustained decreases in seven of the eight possible measurements.[11]

For most economists the wage and pricing behavior just described must seem like economics upside down. The data clearly indicate that recessions and unemployment have not in recent times been effective in reducing average wage increases and, in addition, for the largest firms in concentrated industries have actually resulted in increased markups on direct costs. Restrictive national policies that trigger or accentuate recessions to control inflation are beginning to resemble the use of witchcraft to cure disease. Arthur Burns summed up the foregoing statement (written for this book three years before) very well after the 1980 election. "The sad fact is that in spite of the recession that we have just gone through, the basic rate of inflation is no lower now [November 1980] than it was before the recession started. From the standpoint of our inflation problem, we have had a wasted recession."[12]

It is easy to be a critic but much more difficult to answer even one's own criticism. What would be a good policy for inflation-recessions such as those of 1973/74 and 1980? There are no easy answers.

We probably know enough about alleviating the income losses caused by unemployment in recessions. This is a problem that can be made manageable with unemployment compensation, education and training, job training, public service jobs, and income maintenance. It takes some government-appropriated money and some management; both are available or can be obtained.

Inflation is quite another matter. It cannot persist without support from the supply and/or velocity of money (not appropriated money but media of exchange, checkbook money, created by the banking system), and it cannot be cured by monetary restriction that results in an intolerable rate of unemployment because fiscal measures will be taken (or allowed to occur) to alleviate the effects on the unemployed. And as we have seen, it does not stop the wage push.

The other side of the inflation problem is the supply of goods. More production at higher productivity will, over the long term, improve the buying power of money, which means that it will reduce inflation. A restoration of the growth rate in productivity to its 1948-73 average would allow price increases to be reduced by 2 percent per year. But with productivity declining or improving at only a low rate, and wages rising at a rate of 10 percent or more per year, there is a built-in inflation factor that can go on indefinitely and may well accelerate. As the next chapter will demonstrate, improving productivity will require a large increase in investment in plant, equipment, and technological innovation. This process will be inhibited by overdoing high interest rates as the primary instrument for controlling excessive growth in the money supply and as a primary means of dampening inflation. Each new cost-saving or supply-creating piece of plant or equipment must earn a profit higher than the combined interest rate, risk premium, and extra cost of underdepreciation. In the longer run, investments of this type will reduce costs and permit prices to stabilize or even to be lowered. Each ratchet upward of interest rates – rates in the 10 to 12 percent range, and through the teens in 1979 and 1980 – influences investment decisions toward lower risk, higher return, and faster return of capital. Thus, National Steel chose to shift investment away from new or improved steel-making facilities to acquisition of a finance company, and Mobil bought Marcor.

The head of a firm commenting on the thesis of Chapter 4 wrote:

> In our own subsidiaries we have been systematically eliminating capital-requiring companies for years. We have closed plants and subcontracted manufacturing by changing business methods. In essence we are doing what [Neal's paper suggests] is going on in the economy – the liquidation of capital-intensive industry. . . . It seems to us that . . . policies are unlikely to change and that the elimination of capital-requiring companies will continue. If this is the case, this decision will, over time, steadily eliminate the number of blue-collar jobs, as has been noted by various authors.

There are many ways of squeezing down the wage-price spiral, which constitutes the hard core of the problem of continuing inflation. Models using incomes policies, including tax rebates to encourage moderation of wage increases and tax surcharges for firms and workers who exceed permissible (for example, noninflationary) wage increases abound and give much pleasurable excitement to meetings of economists and government policy makers. They give excruciating pain in unmentionable places to most business executives and labor leaders.

If executives of the largest companies and the largest unions could relieve the pain by agreeing on the least objectionable means of controlling wage and price increases while stimulating productivity, wage-cost-push inflation might be contained. Government people have so badly managed their relations with these groups that a Labor-Management Council appointed by President Richard Nixon severed its government relationship entirely. Yet government cannot be left out, because anything the other two groups (business executives and labor leaders) agree upon will call for government action of one kind or another.

These three groups together have the power to design and to cooperate in an effective program to stop inflation that would have a good chance of being accepted. It may not be the best way to solve the country's greatest economic problem, but sober consideration of the nation's power structure and the nature and intractability of the problem of inflation call for that conclusion. If the three groups do not try, or if they try and fail, then the prospect for controlling inflation in a democratic society is dismal. But recognizing that the three elements of the nation's leadership are responsible will be the first step toward an ultimate accountability for all three. (In the last chapter, we shall return to the subject of how the power groups might be brought together.)

ENTER REAGANOMICS

As this book was going to press, the first Reagan budget and tax proposals for a new beginning for the lagging and inflation-burdened economy were presented to Congress. Paradoxically, they reflected in general major economic promises made during the campaign to reduce taxes and the size and scope of the federal government's role in the economy. This unusual phenomenon in itself, regardless of the merit of the proposals, represents a step toward responsible party politics.

The tax, budget, and other economic proposals directed toward stimulating economic growth may turn out to be inconsistent with controlling inflation. Some proposals are directed toward revitalizing the economy, such as deregulation and tax reductions for individuals and business, and some toward reducing the role of government in the economy by budget and tax cuts and reductions in government loan and loan guarantee programs. But the proposals add up to negligible reductions from the current level of the government deficit to $55 billion for fiscal 1981 and $45 billion for fiscal 1982.

In their own unstructured way, the proposals cut across most of the important macroeconomic policy problems that are major concerns of this book. They are, moreover, based upon only partially stated premises about the structure of the U.S. economy that are considerably different from those that this book makes painfully explicit.

Fortunately, the new administration's short-term macroeconomic proposals concerned with curbing inflation and stimulating investment do not depend heavily upon a correct assessment of the real structure of the economy. Budget cuts and tax cuts in a combination that produces a federal budget surplus would be good medicine for inflation and could result in a healthy reduction in inflationary expectations. The fiscal policy prescription for inflation so often repeated in these pages can be filled by sizable surpluses with or without tax cuts. But no such surpluses are envisioned, even on a high employment basis.

The major importance of the proposed reform of the tax treatment of depreciation is to stimulate investment, improve productivity, and bring about a higher growth rate. As is emphasized in these pages, making up for the erosion of capital caused by inflation and unwise tax policies is a high priority need both to foster growth and to control inflation. It would do both more effectively if other tax cuts were deferred or kept low enough to avoid deficits in fiscal 1981, 1982, and 1983.

Implicitly, the projected deficits will throw upon monetary policy the major burden of carrying the fight against inflation. The resulting tight monetary policy and high interest rates could work at cross purposes to the investment stimulus of depreciation reform. Reducing the amounts or delaying the proposed individual income tax cuts would overcome such inconsistencies. Restructuring the proposed depreciation reforms would reduce their cost in lost tax revenues without a corresponding lessening of their stimulus to building new plant and equipment (as distinguished from buying from the existing stock).

The purpose of this section will have been served if it leaves the impression that, far from being made obsolete by Reaganomics, this book can provide intellectual tools for evaluating the new ideology as it becomes better articulated and more explicit.

NOTE ON A NEGLECTED STABILIZER: EXPORTS

Export policy can become for the United States an important part of its antirecession employment policy. This proposition is well accepted by our competitors but has no status in this country. Whatever we believed earlier about the separation of employment and trade policies deserves reconsideration. Other industrial countries use export-led expansionary policies. Because the United States accounted for a major part of world trade, that option was not open to us 20 to 30 years ago, but our relative decline in economic power makes it available now.

Export policies in other industrial countries are accompanied by tax systems designed to give special push to exports. The value-added taxes of Europe (15 to 20 percent) and heavy excises in Japan are rebated on exports and added on to the prices of imports. This is the result of a General Agreement on Tariffs and Trade (GATT) rule that proclaims indirect taxes to be passed on (and therefore rebatable on exports), whereas direct taxes, mainly our own 48 percent corporate income tax, cannot be rebated because of the contention that they are not passed on, an argument accepted by few economists and even fewer business executives. The Domestic International Sales Corporation (DISC) was installed in the United States partly to offset this unequal treatment by deferring indefinitely a portion of the corporate income tax payable on profits from exports.

In considering stabilization policies to this point, most attention has been given to fiscal and monetary policies. But private investment and foreign trade also have a large role to play; the erratic performance of either or both can require large offsets from the side of fiscal policy.

The changed international position of the United States has brought about some significant and inadequately noted changes in these components of the GNP.

1. Whereas business fixed investment expenditures were double the value of exports in 1950, exports now amount to nearly the same amount annually as business fixed investment, each being equal to about 10 percent of the GNP, and both amounting to two or three times the annual amount of residential construction.
2. Whereas in 1976 nearly half of U.S. imports consisted of fuels (29 percent), minerals and metals (9.5 percent), and agricultural products (9.4 percent) — all of which are complementary to, not competitive with, U.S. employment — more than 76 percent of U.S. exports were in manufactures, which are large generators of employment.
3. There is increasing evidence that changes in exports tend to move in an offsetting direction to changes in GNP and to gross private investment; that is, exports tend to move in a stabilizing way relative to GNP and investment. Thus exports can be something of an automatic stabilizer. This is a concept given little attention by policy makers; it is an idea worthy of much more study.

As to the effects of investment and exports on aggregate demand, each in traditional theory has a multiplier that, in crude language, derives from income generated without a corresponding flow of finished goods onto the domestic market. In a recession, exports and investment become absorbers of credit and savings that would otherwise restrain aggregate demand. Their net effects on total demand and employment would seem to depend on how the two are financed. If investment is financed primarily from internal sources and exports by imports, there is little to choose between them as stimulators of aggregate demand. But if exports are primarily financed by credits, exports can become a powerful stimulant to income and employment. There must be something to this thesis or why would countries such as Japan, the United Kingdom, and West Germany pursue the export-led recovery?

The net employment-stimulating effects of the three major weapons against recession — government expenditures, foreign trade, and domestic private investment — depend very much on how they are financed.

Government expenditure effects are usually the biggest, the most studied, and the most used. In a recession that is not accompanied by a counterrecession increase in government expenditures or by tax cuts, the progressive deficit owing to declining tax receipts (especially from corporations) and increased unemployment compensation (and Supplementary Unemployment Benefits where available) serves to moderate the decline. In these circumstances the government deficit is usually financed by borrowing, and the banking system substitutes government securities for business loans being paid off. There is no stimulus from this, but there is a moderation of the decline because personal income is maintained and credit contraction from declining bank loans is offset by increased bank financing of government debt. A net employment stimulus is also provided by tax cuts and increased public employment, which increase the deficit beyond what would otherwise occur.

The decline in business investment accentuates a recession and is usually accompanied by a payoff of bank and other loans. To provide an offset, governments are led to provide public works, tax cuts, investment credits, and similar stimulants financed by government deficits.

Usually left out of this catechism in the United States is the stimulation of exports. Apparently, what has happened in recent years of slack new private investment is a strong shift toward exports by companies able to make it. But as other industrial countries move in the same direction — toward expanding exports — the net effect of foreign trade changes on employment in the United States can be offset by imports. If, on balance, the United States can increase exports more than imports, the effect will be an expansion of employment. This effect can also be achieved by shifting toward the financing of exports by larger and longer credits. If not so financed, the need of foreigners to pay will increase the demand for dollars abroad, which will appreciate the dollar and raise foreign currency prices of U.S. exports.

In the 1975-77 period, far from appreciating because of strong U.S. exports, the dollar depreciated and the yen and the mark appreciated, partly in a classic response to Japanese and German export surpluses. Clearly, the stimulus to foreign exporters was stronger than the stimulus to U.S. exporters for a variety of reasons, including the fact that the U.S. economic recovery was faster and greater than that of Japan or Germany. It is these countries that obtained the classic expansion of their economies from export-led recoveries, but at the expense of a U.S. increase in imports far in excess of its increase in exports. That increase in U.S. imports, while it may have been antiinflationary, tended to depress employment in many sectors.

The relatively smaller ratio of U.S. exports to world exports has opened an avenue for expanding the U.S. domestic economy, which did not exist when the U.S. economy was relatively much more important. Instead of concentrating antirecession measures only on fiscal policy and investment incentives, the United States can (like Japan and Germany) put added emphasis on exports in a recession. It should do this not by curtailing imports, which would raise consumer and business costs, but by reinforcing its tax and credit incentives to exporters. Avoidance of a growing import surplus by maintaining or increasing exports in recessions would be helpful to the recovery of the U.S. economy. It would offset the export drives by other countries to stimulate their exports to the United States, which appear to be capable of throwing us into large trade deficits — excesses of imports over exports — especially when a large part of our import bill is for oil.

To add export expansion to our arsenal of ways to maintain or stimulate employment will require the adoption or strengthening of policies for that purpose. These include tax incentives for investment in export industries, expansion of export credit on easier terms, and exchange rate policies that lean against temporary appreciation of the dollar as exports improve. Such a policy need not be deterred by the possibility that our export expansion might be most effective with the developing countries. They desperately need, but do not produce, the goods that we most want to export to them and would welcome easier credit during recessions.

NOTES

1. From a personal conversation in the middle 1950s. The principle appears in Ruml's lectures and in CED policy statements.
2. J. M. Keynes, *The General Theory of Employment, Interest and Money* (New York: Harcourt Brace, 1936); John A. Hobson, *The Economics of Unemployment* (London: Allen and Unwin, 1931); William T. Foster and Waddill Catchings, *Money*, 3rd ed. (Boston and New York: Houghton Mifflin, 1927).
3. Committee for Economic Development, *Taxes and the Budget* (New York: CED, 1947).
4. Committee for Economic Development, *Fighting Inflation and Promoting Growth* (New York: CED, 1976).
5. Committee for Economic Development, *Budgeting for National Objectives* (New York: CED, 1966).
6. Committee for Economic Development, *A Stabilizing Federal Budget for 1967* (New York: CED, 1966).
7. As to whether Congress or the Federal Reserve was more likely to be "gutless," the Fed surely deserved little praise for this period, in which I was an associate economist of the Open Market Committee. Sometime before the "accord" of 1951 (the exact date is not available for a reason that will be apparent), all the senior economists of the system were called together for an off-the-record meeting to consider what should be done about continued support by the Fed of the structure of prices of government securities, a practice that had begun at the Fed's initiative when the United States went to war in 1941. We economists had no trouble reaching agreement. So far as open market operations were concerned, the Fed had become an engine of inflation and would remain so if it continued to support the prices of government securities. We agreed unanimously on a report to that effect to be presented to the Open Market Committee. Shortly after we returned to our respective home bases, we were each quietly called and instructed to return our copy of the report and to destroy any record that we might have made of the meeting.

Thomas McCabe, a long-time trustee of the CED and for a time its chairman, took over as Fed chairman in 1948. Despite the desire of President Truman and Treasury Secretary John Snyder to have continued Fed support of government securities, McCabe negotiated an accord with the Treasury to give up the support program. The Treasury's negotiator, William McC. Martin who was in agreement with McCabe on restoring a free market for government securities, soon took over as chairman of the Federal Reserve and the long crisis was ended. Only then could monetary policy begin to play its full role in stabilization – a role that proved to be less effective than had been hoped.
8. See "How Much Stimulus," *New York Times*, January 10, 1975, p. 36.
9. Two policy statements reflecting some of the lessons we learned from the "Nixonomics" period were Committee for Economic Development, *A New U.S. Farm Policy for Changing World Food Needs* (New York: CED, 1974); and idem, *Fighting Inflation and*

Promoting Growth (New York: CED, 1976). Neither in these nor in later statements was a tax-based incomes policy accepted.

10. Howard M. Wachtel and Peter D. Adelsheim, "How Recession Feeds Inflation: Price Markups in a Concentrated Economy," *Challenge*, September-October 1977, pp. 6-14.

11. These results parallel those that I obtained in a study of the same problem for the Great Depression. Compare Alfred C. Neal, *Industrial Concentration and Price Inflexibility* (Washington, D.C.: American Council on Public Affairs, 1942). For that severe depression the average markup of all three groups declined, but the decline was less for high- than for low-concentration industries.

12. Arthur Burns, "Some Advice for Ronald Reagan," *New York Times*, November 16, 1980, sec. 3, p. 3.

4

THE EROSION OF
BUSINESS CAPITAL:
ROLES OF INFLATION,
TAXATION, AND INDOLENCE

Investment by foreigners in the United States has increased enormously in recent years, usually through purchase of companies or plants, not by building new ones. Starved for capital, large U.S. firms, too, have found it increasingly more advantageous to buy up other companies than to invest in their own existing plants. The reason is obvious: it is cheaper to buy than to build. These developments are responses to a long-continued deterioration in the financial structure of the United States.

The market value of net corporate assets measures this malaise. Whereas in most of the 20 years before 1974 corporate market value (equity plus interest-bearing debt) had exceeded current replacement costs of net assets, beginning in 1974 the ratio dropped to 0.666 and stood at 0.561 at the end of 1979.[1] Corporate assets as a whole in 1980 could be bought at a discount of one-third from their replacement cost.

Malaise in the U.S. economy during the 1970s was marked by inflation, a shift to declining and then to negative growth rates in productivity, lagging investment in new plants and equipment, and common stock prices at distress levels. This situation led the Securities Exchange Commission (SEC) and the Financial Accounting Standards Board (FASB) to require that large companies provide an estimate of how their statements would have been affected if depreciation and inventory values were to reflect current rather than historical costs.

The author gratefully acknowledges permission to reprint in this chapter parts of his article that appeared originally as "Immolation of Business Capital," in the *Harvard Business Review*, March-April 1978, © 1978 by the President and Fellows of Harvard College; and parts of a chapter in *Productivity: Prospects for Growth*, ed. Jerome M. Rosow, © 1981 by Litton Educational Publishing, Inc. Reprinted by permission of Van Nostrand Reinhold Company.

The results were almost astonishing. The FASB recommended adjustment for inflation of financial statements for 1979, and the SEC 10-K statements called for similar adjustments, both on an information basis. Table 3 shows the effects on profits of these adjustments for the top 20 of the *Fortune* 500 companies. All, as might be expected, showed much smaller profits — from 24 percent to 68 percent smaller — than those reported without the inflation adjustment. The two companies on the list having losses showed an increase in losses of 33 and 114 percent. These illustrative adjustments for particular companies can be expanded to show the effects of nonfinancial corporations as a whole.[2]

TABLE 3
Net Income of the Top 20 Companies of the FORTUNE 500, 1979 (in millions of dollars)

Company	As Reported in Financial Statements (historical costs)	With Costs and Depreciation Adjusted for General Inflation	Percent Difference
Exxon	4295	3052	−29
General Motors	2893	1776	−39
Mobil	2007	1134	−43
Ford	1169	375	−68
Texaco	1759	930	−47
Standard Oil of California	1785	1309	−27
Gulf Oil	1322	649	−51
IBM	3011	2247	−25
General Electric	1409	1064	−24
Standard Oil of Indiana	1507	1111	−26
IT&T	701	313	−55
Atlantic Richfield[a]	1166	827	−29
Shell Oil	1126	778[b]	−31
U.S. Steel	(383)	(818)	+11.4
Conoco	815	538	−34
Du Pont	939	421	−55
Chrysler	(1097)	(1462)	+33
Tenneco	571	275	−52
Western Electric[a]	636	211	−67
Sun	700	344	−51

[a]From 10-K Reports to SEC.
[b]December 1979 dollars.

Source: From 1979 annual report of each company, except where noted above.

UNDERCOSTING AND EROSION OF CAPITAL

The effect of antique cost-recovery allowances under U.S. tax laws, and of inventory undercosting pursued voluntarily by business, has been an enormous dissipation of capital. Undercosting of inventory and depreciation not only over-states profits and understates losses but gives the wrong signals for both the direction and the volume of investment. Overstated profits have led to payment of excessive income taxes, to frequent payment of dividends that were in excess of real profits, and to starvation of internal sources of funds for investment.

Business has experienced a serious deterioration in its ability to retain internally generated funds that have accounted for the bulk of its financing of plants and equipment. In the four years — 1969 through 1972 — that preceded the most recent surge of inflation, depreciation and retained earnings generated three-fourths of the cash that nonfinancial companies invested in plant, equip-ment, inventory, and mineral rights. As will be shown, in subsequent years the result of undercosting inventories and depreciation seriously undermined the capacity to finance investment from internal sources. Not surprisingly, the growth rate of real fixed capital of business per employee fell by more than 1 percent a year in the 1975-78 period after averaging an increase of more than 2 percent per year in the preceding decade.

Table 4 summarizes major differences between reported and inflation-adjusted results for nonfinancial corporations in the period 1968 through 1979.

In a period of high inflation, depreciation allowed for tax purposes based on original cost and specified useful life falls increasingly short of recovering enough to replace plants and equipment. Inventory costing based on FIFO (first in, first out) does the same with respect to inventory sold, but in this case the fault lies with business because it is permitted to use LIFO (last in, first out), but only about one-third of the inventory of nonfinancial corporations is on LIFO costing. When reported profits, taxes, and retained earnings (after payment of dividends) are corrected for these shortcomings, it is apparent that nonfinancial corporations in the period 1968 through 1979 have paid taxes at much higher rates than reported; have paid a much higher proportion of after-tax profits as dividends than they reported (in 1974 nonfinancial business as a whole paid dividends in excess of after-tax adjusted-for-inflation profits); and have realized retained earnings $240 billion less than they would have if they had not under-costed inventory, had been allowed to depreciate plants and equipment at current cost, and had not in consequence overpaid income taxes.

Capital dissipation from the causes identified increased greatly in 1973 and the years following — the same years that were marked by a slowdown and decline in productivity growth. Retained earnings were about $14 billion below the full-costing optimum for the five-year period preceding 1973 but $161.5 billion below in the five-year period after 1973. The $161.5 billion of potential unrealized earnings retention in the second five-year period amounted to about a year and a third of plants and equipment investment at the rate prevailing in the

TABLE 4
Nonfinancial Corporations Profits before and after Taxes
and Retained Earnings, Adjusted for Inflation, 1968-79
(in billions of dollars)

Year	Profits before Taxes		Profits after Taxes		Retained Earnings	
	Reported	Adjusted	Reported	Adjusted	Reported	Adjusted
1968	71.9	72.1	38.3	38.5	17.6	17.8
1969	68.4	66.4	35.1	33.1	14.4	12.4
1970	55.1	51.5	27.8	24.2	7.9	4.3
1971	63.3	58.8	33.4	28.9	13.4	8.9
1972	75.9	72.0	42.4	38.5	20.7	16.8
Total 1968-72					74.0	60.2
1973	97.7	75.9	53.1	36.3	29.2	12.4
1974	102.9	59.5	60.2	16.8	34.2	− 9.2
1975	101.3	77.0	60.7	36.4	32.2	7.9
1976	130.2	101.4	77.5	48.4	44.4	15.4
1977	143.5	116.5	83.9	56.9	46.7	19.7
1978	166.1	128.3	97.3	59.5	55.5	17.7
1979	191.1	133.7	115.7	58.3	58.7	11.3
Total 1973-79					300.9	75.2
Total 1974-78					213.0	51.5

Source: Derived from George Terborgh, *Inflation and Profits* (Washington, D.C.: Machinery and Allied Products Institute, 1980).

period. It amounted to an annual average about 2.5 times the so-called tax expenditures provided in the tax laws in favor of corporations.

The full effect of the $240 billion deficiency in retained earnings from 1968 through 1979, which was not available for investment, was much greater than the amount implies. This sum was in equity funds, which management can more readily use for risk investment in innovations than it can borrowed funds.

There are secondary effects of undercosting that are worse than paying taxes on profits not really there and dividends not justified by real earnings. One is encouragement of wage increases beyond productivity gains. The effect of overstated profits on labor negotiations is obvious. Companies that are reporting large − albeit illusory − profits can seemingly afford large wage increases. To the upward pressure on prices from externally imposed oil price increases and depreciation of the dollar must be added the pressure of wage increases that are not even partially offset by productivity gains. Just to stay in business under such pressures, companies must raise prices. They have no choice.

The whole process has planted an unexploded bomb. Overstatement of profits triggers adverse public, labor, and political reactions to price increases. Rising costs that reflect the replacement of productivity gains by productivity losses, accompanied by wage increases to catch up with inflation, drain off the real earnings, which in major industries can be only partially restored by price increases.

DECLINE OF U.S. COMPETITIVENESS IN THE WORLD

The deterioration of our economic strength in recent years compounds a long-term decline in our competitiveness in the world. Other countries have had a more rapid rate of growth in world trade. In 1960 the United States accounted for 14.9 percent of world exports; by 1978 that proportion had dropped to 10.9 percent. By contrast, in 1960 we accounted for 11.5 percent of imports from the rest of the world, whereas in 1978 we were taking 13.5 percent. Obviously, the United States has become a better country in which to sell and a poorer country from which to buy. The record of Japan offers an interesting contrast. In 1960 Japan accounted for 4.2 percent of world exports, but by 1978 its share was 7.5 percent and still going up. Growth of its share of world imports paralleled at a lower level the increase in its share of world exports.

Considerable understanding of the deterioration of U.S. economic strength in the world can be gained by comparing its rate of investment and growth with that of its principal competitors. Table 5 compares average savings rates for corporations (depreciation and retained earnings) and individuals for the period 1960 through 1977 with growth in gross domestic product (GDP) per civilian employee (a measure of productivity). The data clearly indicate that higher savers are faster growers in productivity, with the United States lowest in productivity growth and close to the bottom in its savings ratio.[3]

INVESTMENT INADEQUATE FOR GROWTH

On the surface, it might appear that the volume of investment was not a factor in explaining declining growth and productivity. Gross business plant and equipment investment in relation to gross business product has since 1945 remained close to an average of 10 percent. This ratio holds even after deduction of investments for environmental protection. But the relatively well-maintained ratio of gross business investment to GNP is misleading. A large part of such investment must be devoted to replacing worn-out plants and equipment and used-up inventory. When these replacements, valued at current cost, were subtracted from gross investment, it was found that a diminishing proportion of investment had been devoted to making additions of new physical capital. In the five years ending 1969, net new investment (after subtracting the current cost of replacements from gross investment) was nearly 64 percent of the total.

TABLE 5

Average Ratio of Corporate and Household Savings to Gross
Domestic Product and Average Annual Growth in Real Gross
Domestic Product per Employee, 1960-77
(in percent)

Country	Savings Rate	Growth, Gross Domestic Product, per Civilian Employee
Japan	29.7	7.6
Italy	25.5	4.5
Belgium	22.3	3.9
Netherlands	22.2	3.8
Germany	21.0	4.0
France	20.5	4.0
Canada	19.0	2.0
United States	16.5	1.5
United Kingdom	14.9	2.3
Sweden	14.1	2.1

Source: Analysis by author of data from Organization for Economic Cooperation and Development, in "Savings Levels and Productivity Growth," *Capital Goods Review* (Washington, D.C.: Machinery and Allied Products Institute, 1980).

In the five years ending 1978, this ratio of net additions to capital stock had fallen to 49 percent. Thus, net additions of new physical capital to the total stock fell drastically in the 1970s.

There are some other disturbing trends in the pattern of U.S. investment. World War II gave enormous impetus to research and technological advance in the United States as well as to many types of new industrial investment. (Some, of course, adapted from work in other countries.) One needs only to name nuclear fission, computers, radar, space exploration, communications satellites, microwave and laser beam transmission, and volume production of civilian and military jet engine aircraft. With its industrial base undamaged by war and peacetime markets eager to be served, at the end of the war the United States was prepared for and enjoyed two decades of technological and industrial supremacy. In this period Western European countries and Japan caught up technologically in fields where they had lagged. They began to make advances of their own while the United States reduced its rate of growth in government research and development (R&D) expenditures. While the ratio of industrial investment to gross output in the United States was maintained, as has been noted, its effect upon economic growth after the mid-1960s was due almost entirely to labor and capital inputs, not to extra efficiencies resulting from advances in management and application of innovations derived from government-financed research.[4] Restoring the productivity growth rate calls not only for more investment but for a better allocation to uses embodying new technology and higher efficiency. In particular, the subsidies that induce an over-allocation of capital to housing have not yet been offset by tax changes for business that would permit recovery of the replacement cost of plants and equipment.[5] Governments of most other industrial countries have long permitted this in one way or another, not the least of which is heavy reliance on indirect taxation rather than on corporate profits taxes.

PRODUCTIVITY DECLINE AND CAPITAL INVESTMENT

Sooner or later the deficient rate and misallocation of fixed capital investment in the United States was destined to show up in a reduced rate of growth in productivity and a reduced standard of living. While it would be reckless to attribute to this one source all of the recent deterioration of the nation's output per person and decline in real income, it would be gross negligence not to look to this source as a major contributing cause. Let us examine the record.

It is a commonplace truth that investment in capital goods, in technological research, and in education and training share the same precondition in a period of high employment: the forgoing of current consumption (or production for current consumption) and the use of the economic resources so diverted to provide goods or services that are usable only in future periods. In considering the question of improving productivity, therefore, the contribution of capital investment can take tangible or intangible form. Capital can be embodied in physical form (plants, equipment, and inventories) or in human form (improvement of knowledge, education, and training). While comparable data are not available on the productivity of all forms of investment, some of the most important information is.

It is useful to consider briefly the role that capital investment has played in the decline in productivity in recent years. Using a 1979 summary of sources of productivity growth (national income per person employed),[6] the contribution of capital by sources selected to match the definition above in the 1948-73 period accounted for 2.73 percent annual growth in productivity, or more than the net annual average growth rate from all sources per person employed of 2.43 percent (see Table 6).

There was an unprecedented decline in the growth rate of productivity per person in the 1973-76 period from the 1948-73 average, a change from +2.43 to −0.54, a drop of nearly three percentage points.

The largest influence in the total decline was in "advances in knowledge and miscellaneous determinants," which dropped from +1.41 to −0.75. This is a category that is not self-explanatory. Denison notes that "capital input is so defined and measured that changes in output that result from advances in the

TABLE 6
Growth Rates and Selected Sources of Growth, in National Income per Person Employed, 1948-73 and 1973-76 (in percent)

	1948-73	1973-76
Growth Rate (annual average, all sources)	2.43	−0.54
Selected contributions to growth rates, percentage points:		
Education	0.52	0.88
Inventories	0.10	0.02
Nonresidential structures and equipment	0.29	0.25
Economies of scale	0.41	0.24
Advances in knowledge and miscellaneous determinants	1.41	−0.75
Total contribution of selected sources	2.73	0.64

Source: Derived from Edward F. Denison, "Explanations of Declining Productivity Growth," *Survey of Current Business 59*, no. 8 (August 1979): p. 3.

design of capital goods are classified as contributions of advances in knowledge, not of capital." Advances in knowledge "measure gains in measured output that result from the incorporation into production of new knowledge of any type — managerial and organizational as well as technological."[7] But this classification is a residual that also includes miscellaneous determinants. So far the factors that account for the large drop in the growth rate of "advances in knowledge and miscellaneous determinants" beginning in 1973 have not been identified in more detail.

It should be clear from the foregoing paragraphs that the role of *capital*, as I have broadly defined it, will be of critical importance in reversing the slowdown in productivity. Of the 3 percent drop in productivity growth from 1948-73 to 1973-76, more than two-thirds was in the capital and "miscellaneous determinants" category shown in Table 6.

The maintenance of gains in "nonresidential structures and equipment" should also not be misunderstood. Changes from economies of scale, from improvements in plants and equipment, and from new products are all included in other categories, not in the "nonresidential structures and equipment" sector as defined.

EFFECTS OF SHOCKS TO THE ECONOMY ON PRODUCTIVITY

A striking feature of the slowing of U.S. productivity growth in the period beginning 1973 was that it was accompanied by (usually) less drastic slowdowns in other industrial countries. Students of the problem have suggested that this is a clue to a common cause or set of causes.

The year 1973 witnessed some major shocks to the United States and world economies. The first and outstanding shock to the world economy was the run-up of oil prices by the Organization of Petroleum Exporting Countries (OPEC). This and a run-up of grain prices triggered a new and large ratchet of inflation in the United States (to a double-digit level) and similar movements elsewhere. A third wave of shocks followed from two earlier devaluations of the dollar and the subsequent shift to a moderated floating exchange rate system. A fourth ripple of shocks emanated from the drastic use of restrictive monetary policies as a response to these inflationary developments, with an ensuing rise in interest rates around the world.

The theoretical consequences of these shocks can easily be sketched. The oil price inflation had far-reaching effects on productivity. These included acceleration of energy conservation, requiring unexpected investment outlays that did not add to productivity, and a step-up in gasoline conservation with consequences on everything from reduced highway speed limits to a sudden increase in investment in equipment for making more energy-efficient automobiles, air conditioners, buildings, and the like.

The change in expectations about inflation and interest rates stirred people to "buy now" with borrowed money those things that were expected to rise most in price. Housing became a primary inflation hedge that soaked up personal savings (and credit usage) that might have gone into other things. Expansion of consumer credit for buying consumer goods also lowered the savings rate. To these changes was added an unknown amount of speculation in gold and silver holdings, land, antiques, and art, which added nothing to productivity.

High and rising interest rates and the expectation of their continuance had important consequences for business investment. For example, corporate bond yields rose from below 8 percent in 1973 to more than 13 percent in 1980, commercial paper had even larger swings, and the prime rate reached 21 percent in 1980. Expected returns on business investment had to be higher to offset higher (implicit) interest rates, the risk of tying up funds in long pay-out projects was increased, and the desirability of short pay-out investments was enhanced. Investment in equipment was favored over structures, and low investment-to-sales uses of capital were favored over high. Mergers shifted investment funds toward acquiring finance and insurance companies, retail merchandising, fast-food chains, and enterprises that were labor intensive. Many heavy per worker investments with long pay-out times — utilities, steel, paper, and chemicals — were deferred or scaled back.

In this process of adjustment, capital was substituted for fuel and energy (again, without improvement in productivity) and labor was substituted for both capital and energy (because wages did not increase nearly as fast as the costs of energy and capital). Substitution took such forms as investing in insulation to save energy and using overtime or adding shifts in manufacturing and processing instead of expanding plants.

Foreign competitors — often U.S.-owned and many equipped with newer and technologically more advanced plants, a consequence of long-continued higher savings and investment rates in their countries — stepped up their sales to the United States despite their appreciated currencies. Export drives abroad were assisted by the rebating of value-added taxes on exports and government-assisted financing. Import competition reduced investment prospects in the United States for such industries as steel and producers' equipment.

Large additions to the labor force of young people and women had productivity-reducing effects, a factor noted by all investigators. Almost unnoted, however, was the increased rate of retirement at earlier ages by older persons whose embodiment of human capital was high. The proportion of male workers between ages 55 and 64 in the labor force dropped from 83 to 74 percent between 1970 and 1977 and is expected to fall to 68 percent by 1985.[8]

It will take a long time to sort out and quantify the effects of the changes described above on U.S. productivity, but I believe it is in such monolithic shifts as those described that the mystery of the disproportionate lowering of U.S. productivity since 1973 will be unraveled. That the role of business capital investment in productivity growth is important has been demonstrated beyond question.

BUSINESS PROPOSALS TO IMPROVE INVESTMENT

For the short-term future, the knee-jerk reaction of business to undercosting and lagging investment is to raise prices. Higher prices will improve both profitability and internal cash flows, which can then be invested. If workers, the public, OPEC, and the U.S. government all stood still for this, it would be a serious, if unconscionable, option. Knowledge gained from recent history leads us to expect little from going this route but a savage conflict over income shares. Which groups get higher incomes? Which pay higher prices? Which become unemployed? The battle to maintain living standards as prices rise faster than wages and salaries has set class against class and sector against sector. The drive to maintain markets has thrust us into conflict with foreign economies. The second bout of double-digit inflation and high unemployment, beginning in late 1979, threatened to destroy the society we have known.

An important option for resolving the dilemma of restoring an adequate rate of investment without inflation is to go to one source of the problem: taxation. Much of what follows is about that option. With the administration and Congress pledged to making tax reforms to stimulate growth, business organizations should have had ready plans to rescue capital investment from undercosting in order to restore growth in productivity.

It occurred to me that perhaps organizations of business people had begun forthrightly to reject the totems of the past — double taxation of dividends, lower capital gains taxes, across-the-board cuts in corporate taxes, improving depreciation allowances, and balancing the federal budget at lower expenditure levels. In 1977 I asked good friends in the National Association of Manufacturers, the U.S. Chamber of Commerce, the Business Roundtable, and other organizations for their swatch of current tax proposals and received some excellent presentations of the capital needs problem but none included a recommendation for current cost depreciation or even wider use of LIFO inventory costing.

THE CED ON CAPITAL RECOVERY

The business executives in the CED,[9] one would suppose, should have been in the forefront of those hammering out practical, workable policy proposals. Probably no problem of such magnitude has been addressed by the CED's trustees with as much ambivalence as that of capital erosion. In a path-breaking policy statement early in the postwar period, the CED outlined its stabilizing budget policy (which is discussed in Chapter 3) and its postwar tax reform proposals.[10]

The first and boldest statement of the CED's depreciation philosophy was made just after World War II by a group who had lived through and fought the tightening of Treasury regulations on "useful lives" for depreciable assets. Said the committee in its 1947 statement, "within the limits of reason, business management should be permitted to use its own judgment in establishing depreciation rates." The committee did not comment on the possibility that adoption of this proposal might lead to bunching of purchases of capital goods in years of high profits to be charged off immediately or on the possible destabilizing effect of this practice on the federal budget and on the economy. Its view did, however, obviate much need to talk about replacement-cost depreciation; the option to use any method to charge off total investment would take care of that.

From this first sweeping demand for free depreciation followed several years of retrogression. Seven years later, in 1954, the committee was merely arguing for shorter useful lives and more depreciation in the early years, a perennial proposal revived in the Capital Cost Recovery Act of 1980.

But the CED met and failed to recognize its opportunity for greatness in this area in 1960. With the advent of the Kennedy administration, implementing the presidential promise to get the country moving again clearly called for finding and putting into place tax reforms that would replace obstacles to growth with incentives. The CED boldly defined the issue in its 1961 policy statement, *Growth and Taxes.* "Investment has a crucial role in the process of economic growth. . . . The high tax rates curtail the funds available to business from internal sources."[11] Priority over a general tax cut should be given, said the CED, to adjustments in depreciation, since the tax reduction from the higher depreciation allowances that they proposed on new investment would go exclusively to firms making expenditures on new buildings, plants, and equipment.

The statement then moved on to current cost depreciation. It considered (but rejected) the possibility of allowing taxpayers to adjust depreciation charges for changes in prices to keep intact the real value or physical productivity of capital. This thrust toward current cost depreciation, it must be noted, came primarily from executives of heavy-investment industries, not those from the financial or service sectors nor from the economic advisers. The point obviously came under hot dispute (unhappily missing from the archives). The record reveals only that in the middle of the usual final mail vote on the completed policy statement containing the negative conclusion just quoted, a revised version of the depreciation recommendation was sent out for a special vote.

The language of the suggested revision was strong and unmistakable, and its sponsors turned out to be prophets with second sight. Remember they were speaking out in 1960. The alternative proposed was drastic.

"As long as depreciation of property is limited to its historical cost, no likely degree of acceleration [faster write-off] can compensate for the erosion of capital brought about by the presently experienced inflation. It is a matter of extreme importance to businesses with heavy investments in property that depreciation allowances . . . should be adjusted for price-level changes, particularly if the urgent need for future growth is to be met." Depreciation geared to changes in the price level "is needed to prevent the confiscation of capital in the guise of a tax on income, and it would still be needed even if inflation were stopped now." There followed a recommendation that the tax laws be changed to "permit adequate and timely depreciation allowances . . . that recognize fully changes in the purchasing power of the dollar."

The policy statement solemnly recorded that "the majority of this Committee does not believe that at the present time revision of the tax treatment of depreciation to allow adjustment for price level changes should be included in the limited category of urgent and feasible tax revision to which this statement is addressed."

In 1974, as inflation raged, the CED undertook once again to look at the problem of capital erosion and capital needs and established a committee to produce a policy statement on meeting capital needs. The project was shelved quietly without even the formality of putting its proposals to a vote. In a January 1980 statement it revived its old standby, accelerated depreciation, which could at the time mean little else than endorsement of 10-5-3 in the Capital Cost Recovery Act of 1980.[12]

WHO PAYS THE CORPORATE INCOME TAX?

Proposals for tax reforms to stimulate investment and growth must run a gauntlet of competing but strongly held positions of business groups, labor organizations, public interest organizations, and economists. Among these are balancing the budget at a reduced rate of expenditure, cutting the corporate income tax, substituting a value-added tax for all or part of the corporate tax, eliminating so-called double taxation of corporate profits, improving the rate of personal savings, and many others. Many proposals are premised on a theory of who pays the corporate profits tax, a subject on which public finance theories of economists come into conflict with business philosophy and practice. The conflict of theories is well illustrated by the argument that corporate dividends are subject to double taxation, once when earned by the company and a second time when stockholders are taxed on dividends received.

It is often argued that if stockholders own the company, they also own the profits that it earns and should pay the taxes on them. According to that reasoning, the corporate profits tax should be eliminated.[13] It is argued that to tax corporate profits and then to tax dividends derived from them is double taxation. (By contrast, partnerships are taxed but once on the profits realized by the partners.)

If stockholders were taxed on all corporate reported profits, paid or not paid out, the pressure to include all costs, and current cost depreciation, would become almost irresistible. But there is very little support for the full integration into one tax of both corporate and personal income taxes on profits. Such an integrated tax on profits would put great pressure on companies to pay out most or all profits and decrease retained earnings. But retention of earnings by companies does not rob stockholders. It adds to company net worth and should eventually lead to higher values for shareholders' stock that would be subject only to a capital gains tax on the increased value of the stock. By the same argument, dissipation of capital by undercosting inventories and depreciation results in overpayment of dividends and taxes and deprives shareholders of possible capital gains.

The root of the trouble over double taxation of profits is a misguided concept of the nature of corporate profits and of who pays the tax on them. Because I believe that the "tax expenditure" for relieving so-called double taxation of profits might better be used to relieve the erosion of physical capital, I will devote a little space to the principles involved in the argument.

In a purely competitive economic system − one wherein many sellers of each product compete with each other and therefore sell at the lowest prices they can afford and still stay in business − some sellers will be covering only their costs (including a market rate of return on capital) and would make no returns beyond that except as management income, equivalent to salary. Only those fortunate sellers with total costs lower than prices would realize a profit, something over and above what is necessary to keep them in business. Such profit is a *surplus*, a return (by definition) above what is really needed to keep the marginal seller's supply coming to market. A tax on such profit is a tax on a surplus and cannot be passed on to others. If most such profits are taxed away, there will be no change in supply, but sellers having to pay the profits tax would probably have to replace the retained earnings that were taxed away by borrowing.

The business executive's view of profits is quite different from seeing it as a true surplus (or rent). The name of the game that companies play is the bottom line. After the company has paid all its costs and its taxes, what is left is profits. What keeps the company going is the rate of return that these after-tax profits provide on invested capital, net worth. For a growing economy, the rate of return on invested capital has to be high enough not only to retain capital in the company but to attract additional capital for financing additional investment in plants, equipment, and working capital. In a growing economy, the after-tax return on the company's investment must be at least equal to returns it could get by investing elsewhere: in other companies or other countries or by liquidation and placement of the proceeds into loans, real estate, securities, or other investments (as some companies have done).

Executives continually maintain that products are necessarily priced to bring a satisfactory return after taxes. This means that the corporate profits tax is passed on, usually in prices that are unnecessarily high because of the pass-on. Because it raises or holds up prices and because it requires higher returns on new investment, the corporate profits tax may be bad for the economy and probably should be reduced even if the revenue loss has to be made up by substituting a broad-based excise or value-added tax to maintain government revenues. Executives see the corporate profits tax and excise taxes as having the same incidence on prices; both are passed on. And a tax that is passed on is not a double tax. The CED's trustees, after embracing the double-taxation argument in 1947, adopted this conclusion in 1962 and have not changed it.[14]

If, as I believe, the foregoing argument is correct, then corporate profits taxes are for the most part not taxes on profits but a part of the cost of doing business. Profits after taxes are a return on equity that, on the average, should be high enough to yield the going rate of return on capital. If it does not earn that much, the market value of equity plus debt will fall below the replacement cost of net assets, a condition that has existed since 1973. That condition is itself a basis for corporate tax relief of some kind.[15]

The mischief done by theorists about the incidence of direct taxes, of which the corporate income tax is one, is causing increasing trouble in international trade. Whereas indirect taxes — for example, value-added or sales taxes — are considered to be passed on fully in prices, the corporate income and other direct taxes are considered by most theorists not to be passed on or to be passed on only in part. Therefore, the value-added tax can be imposed on imports and rebated on exports, whereas no such treatment is permitted for direct taxes. The rebated value-added tax on imports into the United States is being challenged as a subsidy, and the temporary and partial exemption of the corporate tax on U.S. exports (Domestic International Sales Corporation [DISC]) is under attack abroad as an export subsidy. A lot of trouble would be saved if all taxes on producers were considered to be passed on in prices. Thus, the problem of international trade surcharges and subsidies because of domestic tax systems would largely disappear. Where else but from prices, ask business executives, would you get the money to pay taxes?

TAX REFORM TO ESTABLISH CURRENT COST DEPRECIATION

The erosion of physical capital by failing to make financial provision for its renewal can be reduced, and in most cases eliminated, by appropriate tax policies. It cannot be stopped altogether, nor should it be, because companies that do not earn enough will not have a cash counterpart to their depreciation cost and, if that condition continues, will go out of business (as they should).

One part of the tax reform is already in place: the option to use LIFO costing for inventory. While this method results in accelerating the timing of price increases, it does preserve capital invested in inventory. The fact that a majority of companies still do not use LIFO is incomprehensible. Ignorance and unwillingness to take the loss involved in shifting may be partially responsible. Also, some companies may be unable to construct an index for price adjustment acceptable to the Internal Revenue Service.[16] One trustee executive's comment about failure of companies to adopt LIFO was that if he were on the board of such a company, he would consider suing it. None of his colleagues disagreed.

The principle involved in extending current costing to depreciation is similar to that used for inventory. An inflation index could be applied to book costs of structures and equipment annually to put them on an inflation-adjusted basis. It is not necessary to employ cost indexes related to particular classes of capital equipment, structures, and the like because what is needed is only to restore the purchasing power of the dollars frozen into such investments. From the inflation-adjusted book cost, depreciation already taken in prior years would be deducted. The remainder would be the new base, which could be depreciated (using the same depreciation formula) to obtain the current year's depreciation. The same procedure could be repeated in succeeding years if inflation were to continue.

The foregoing is but one of many possibilities. It is often resisted because of opposition in principle to indexing, despite already widespread use of indexing for wages, Social Security, government pensions, inventories (LIFO), commercial space leases, and many other payments and transactions.

If it is firmly expected that inflation will be brought under control, a one-time revaluation of depreciable assets could be carried out with subsequent depreciation being based on the new values. One-time revaluations were commonly used in European countries after major wartime and postwar inflations. This method, however, may result in failure to make up underdepreciation for the years preceding revaluation.

The adoption of current cost depreciation all at once could result in a large increase of cash flow to business and a loss of tax revenue to the Treasury. On a national income accounts basis, the increased cash flow to business could be $20 to $25 billion in the first year (based on 1980 capital consumption adjustment) and a tax loss to the government of about $8 to $10 billion.

Amounts of this size should not upset the economy. If the addition to the federal deficit were deemed excessive, the amount claimed for the inflation adjustment of depreciation could be held in escrow by the Treasury until used by business for capital expenditures, the procedure now followed for the 10 percent investment tax credit.

There are those who will object that this method of increasing investment will work to the advantage of companies already in business and possessing large amounts of depreciable property compared with new business and those having a small ratio of physical capital to sales. This can be admitted; it is true of the investment tax credit and of earlier liberalizations of depreciation. The answer must be "You've got to get it where it's at," to use the new vernacular. Critics should be reminded again that under present conditions it is too often cheaper to buy than to build because sellers cannot obtain anything like current value from depreciation but can obtain some part of it by selling out. It is present, more than proposed, policy that is increasing the concentration of business.

CAPITAL COST RECOVERY AND 10-5-3

Until recently, organizations representing business have been reluctant to face up to the capital erosion problem by supporting current cost depreciation and wider use of LIFO. As the problem became more acute, however, a coalition was formed around a compromise directed at shortening the tax lives of physical assets regardless of their so-called useful lives. This compromise, referred to as 10-5-3 for short, is the proposed Capital Cost Recovery Act of 1979. It provides ten-year depreciation for structures, including commercial real estate, that draws support from manufacturing and construction industries, real estate investors, supermarkets, stores, and service outlets, all of whom have investment concentrated in structures.

Five-year write-offs would be available for equipment, to provide relief for manufacturing and mining as well as for machinery and equipment industries. A three-year write-off providing up to $100,000 for automobiles and trucks attracts the support of small business. These periods of depreciation are all shorter than those now permitted, especially for structures, and the ten-year rule may cause a ballooning of the already large tax shelter in commercial real estate.

It should be noted especially that the shortened depreciation periods proposed apply only to property acquired after January 1, 1980. They would provide no relief for underdepreciation of capital goods already on hand, and this is a major part of the problem.

Shorter lives for depreciable assets will also reduce the bite of future inflation but will not eliminate it. And just as the investment tax credit favored investments in equipment over those in structures, an unbalanced shortening of depreciation periods will favor some lines of investment over others that might make a much greater contribution to improving productivity.

Published estimates of the annual cost of tax revenues to be lost by the Treasury by adopting 10-5-3 are much higher than the tax revenues that might be lost from granting current cost tax treatment to depreciation.[17] Since 10-5-3 does nothing to correct the erosion of existing capital by underdepreciation and seems to be costly in terms of tax revenues lost, it would appear to be a second- or third-best alternative to allowing current cost depreciation. Coupled with the latter, it would be highly desirable although very expensive in terms of tax revenues lost.

THE INVESTMENT TAX CREDIT

The most recent major experiment in tax policy to stimulate investment, now made permanent, is the investment tax credit. A tax credit, first of 7 percent and later of 10 percent, for new investment in equipment (not plants) was inaugurated in 1962 as a countercyclical measure. It was subject to reduction or withdrawal to help stabilize the economy. In its original form, its effect was hard to measure and was much attenuated by uncertainty about when and to what extent it would be available. The credit was made permanent in 1978, and the amount that might be taken was expanded in stages from 50 percent of a company's total tax liability to a top rate of 90 percent of the total tax liability, to become effective in 1982.

The 10 percent tax credit was used to the extent of $8.26 billion in 1977, or about 6.5 percent of that year's expenditures for new equipment. Its value to business in that year was equal to about one-quarter of the year's undercosting of depreciation and inventory. And at current rates of use it would be worth less than one year's inflation in the cost of investment to which it applied. The credit does lower the initial cost of an eligible investment and provides some funds for it, thus raising the rate of return, but it is not known how much investment would have been made anyway without benefit of the credit. It has made funds available that would otherwise have been paid in taxes, but it is clearly not addressed to ending the erosion of capital by undercosting in a period of inflation. Nevertheless, it is a useful stimulant and deserves to be continued.

ALTERNATIVE TAX INCENTIVES FOR INVESTMENT

There are other ways of modifying the tax system to improve the supply of capital to U.S. business. For example, further cuts could be made in the corporate tax rate, capital gains taxes could be further reduced, and incentives to savings such as a tax credit for interest on savings as well as for dividends could be introduced. (It is incorporated in the windfall tax measure adopted early in 1980.) A more fundamental reform such as the substitution of a value-added tax for all or part of the corporate income tax also deserves serious consideration.

All of these proposals suffer from a common defect: they do not directly remedy what is in effect a tax on physical capital imposed by tax laws and regulations limiting capital recovery to original cost — a tax that becomes increasingly onerous as inflation continues. Most proposals, except that for a shift from a corporate income tax to a value-added tax, provide general relief but leave uncorrected the imposition of corporate income taxes on the illusory profits that result from undercosting depreciation and inventory. Tax relief should be targeted to that objective if it is to contribute the most per dollar of reduced tax revenues toward improving productivity.

Substitution of a value-added tax for the corporate income tax would eliminate the tax on capital. Substitution for the corporate income tax of the most common form of the value-added tax, using a consumption base, would impose a value-added tax as a percentage of sales. The taxpayer would remit the tax that is added to sales, reduced by the amount of tax he has paid on purchases. Deduction of the value-added tax paid prevents duplication of the tax as goods pass forward in the production and distribution system and, in the process, offsets any tax paid on capital equipment. Elimination of the tax on capital that is inherent in the corporate income tax would in itself improve corporate cash flow and the supply of investment funds. Promising as the proposal for a value-added tax might seem, its far-reaching effects on the whole tax system — one of which is that the change might make the tax system more regressive — give a low probability to its being adopted soon.

INVESTMENT TAX INCENTIVES AND THE FIGHT AGAINST INFLATION

Depreciation reform, however, should not be undertaken in such a way as to weaken the role of fiscal policy in the fight against inflation. It is inflation, after all, that makes depreciation reform so necessary. Reducing inflation will reduce the loss of tax revenues from depreciation reform. Early in 1980 Congress earmarked about $136 billion from new windfall profits taxes on oil for tax relief in the 1980s. Part of revenues from the windfall profits tax might well be dedicated to depreciation reform. In any event, a fiscal policy that produces a federal budget surplus is an essential complement to depreciation reform.

By making the retirement of government debt possible, budget surpluses would contribute toward three antiinflation objectives. First, a budget surplus would reduce the banking system's holdings of government securities by paying them off and, thereby, would reduce creation of more credit, which adds to inflationary pressures. Second, funds made available to the private sector from retiring government debt, together with accompanying lower interest rates, would provide additional means to finance new investment. Third, increased investment would lower costs and prices (or reduce their rate of increase) and, therefore, over a period of time, would put downward pressure on the price level. Whatever tax reforms are adopted to stimulate investment should be within the context of a fiscal policy aimed at achieving an overall budget surplus, at least under conditions of high employment.

OBSTACLES TO RESTORING THE CAPITAL BASE

Why has understanding fallen so far short of our needs, and why has there been so little demand for policy changes that, I hope, now seem necessary? While much remains unknown or only dimly perceived, there is enough evidence to propose that there are three obstacles our country's leadership must overcome if it is to stop the erosion of our capital base.

The Philosophical Obstacle

The first major obstacle is philosophical. Economists and writers who hold a formalistic view of laissez-faire deny that there is any capital shortage.

Supply and demand will be balanced by the market, they argue. Savings will equal investment as they always have. Let the market work; at some rate of return, investment demand will, if larger than usual, drive up the cost of capital and a higher rate of return will bring forth an increased supply of savings to match the demand already reduced by higher interest rates.

Because it is so familiar and because it fits so well with the philosophical predispositions of business executives who instinctively shrink from advocating government intervention, this view evokes a kind of mental paralysis.

But how can keeping our hands off correct a situation that has worsened because we have been following such a policy? Let me simply recite the main reasons for rejecting formal laissez-fairism.

Socially mandated investment for pollution control, safety, and alternative energy sources will have first call on investable funds and will raise the cost of capital or keep it from falling.

Most major basic industries have been earning rates of return that discourage new plant investment. The higher cost of capital resulting from mandated investment will further discourage "productive" investment. Moreover, cash flow of companies is greatly attenuated by current and prior-year undercosting, which is both reducing their ability to finance their capital needs internally and increasing their demand for loans.

The combination of these two developments will result in strains on capacity and heavy upward pressure on prices as bottlenecks occur in basic industries with long lead times for expanding capacity.

Monetary restriction, the traditional response to an upsurge of loan demand and inflation, will discourage needed investment and will result in an unacceptably high level of unemployment accompanied by unacceptable inflation.

Government will again incur deficits as tax revenues fall and antirecession measures become necessary. Tax reform will again be postponed.

Inexperience of Leaders

The second major obstacle is that political and intellectual leaders have seldom, if ever, had to contend with the problem of maintaining the capital base of civilization.

Our political leaders – former professors, deans, college presidents, officers of the armed forces, civil servants, and lawyers – have all come from long immersion in an environment that makes no provision for replacement and renewal of its capital base.

Consider the following remark from a college treasurer: "It's not a cash expenditure, so it doesn't make any difference whether we leave it out or put it in the budget."

He was talking about an item in the college budget called "equipment replacement reserve." Some of us serving on the school's board of trustees had been fighting to incorporate the reserve in the budget. But we found it hard to impress on the treasurer the importance of including it because no part of his experience or education had brought home to him that expenses to provide for the replacement of capital are just as important as those for current cash outlays.

Almost universally, however, neither educational institutions nor governments – federal, state, or local – make any provision for replacing their capital except when they pay cash for new equipment or buildings. If colleges need money for a new building, they ask a legislative body for it, or have a capital fund drive, or borrow the money. If governments need money for new equipment, they appropriate it from money raised by taxation or by borrowing.

Depreciation, or a reserve for replacing plants and equipment, does not appear in the accounts of the institutions in which our leaders have served. Only in recent years have accountants begun to recommend that nonprofit organizations recognize this cost, but they still do not recommend it for governments or schools.

Moreover, the public does not demand it because few people consider it in their own purchases as consumers. How many cars or houses are bought out of "depreciation reserves"? The sellers of new homes, cars, and major appliances concentrate on how much the buyer has to pay per month to finance the loan for his purchase. When a replacement becomes necessary, it is made by negotiating another loan.

I am not suggesting that depreciation be charged by the consumer on the "plant and equipment" that he owns for personal use; I am only pointing out that people as consumers have no experience with charging the cost of the item as it depreciates so that during the time that the item is useful, the cost of its replacement has been set aside.

The difference is that paying off a loan restores the consumer's credit to go into debt again to replace the worn-out item, but a business cannot operate this way. By the time a company's piece of equipment has worn out, its cost has to be recovered through depreciation charges or the company will be no more. (Obviously the problem is more complicated for the economy as a whole, but the differences are ignored here for simplicity.)

There is some hope that the nation's intellectual leaders will learn something about providing for replacement of capital from their experience with variable annuities and with the application of the principle of maximizing total return on endowment funds. Both became popular in the 1950s and 1960s. Both involved investing in common stocks and counting capital gains and dividends as income.

A few years ago the head of the Ford Foundation castigated endowed colleges for their stodgy investment behavior and low returns compared with those on this new road to riches. The Teachers Insurance and Annuity Association (TIAA), the leading insurer of college pension funds, permitted its clients to invest up to 100 percent of their pension funds in common stocks. Rising stock market prices were expected to compensate for inflation.

But as I look back over the past 15 years, the results are staggering: consumer prices rose 130 percent and the Standard and Poor's 500 index of stock prices (Standard and Poor's index of 500 common stocks) rose 17 percent. Historically, the data indicate that high-grade common stocks have been a good hedge against inflation; the TIAA demonstrated this before offering its variable annuity program. What the studies did not take into account was that companies that pay out part of their capital as dividends and as taxes are not capable of the appreciation in value on which the continued increase in common stock prices depends.

What needs explaining is why the reports of the august and respected financial institutions that educated us in the virtues of growth stocks and maximum total return have yet to diagnose the downfall of their theory. They say nothing, at least in public, about how perniciously contrary to the public interest are the accounting conventions and tax laws that have allowed inflation to erode investments. Perhaps they are reaching the point on their learning curves that would lead them to insist that the leaders of business and government put an end to mass financial rape of prudent people.

Business Neglect

The third major obstacle is one that business leaders have erected themselves. With the administration pledged to make sweeping tax reform proposals soon, business organizations should have ready plans to rescue U.S. capital investment from the dilemma I have described. But they have not been able to agree on any except accelerated depreciation for future investments. And many companies have not even adopted LIFO.

How can we explain this failure of major business groups to face up to a problem on which the future of the business system is balanced? Of course, corporate managers are reluctant to take unilateral action to correct their over-statement of profits, although many have done so in adopting LIFO. But their own collective recommendations for relief from the burden of the corporate income tax provide one clue to an answer: most of their favorite nostrums would not affect reported profits before tax; they would have the overstatement of profits and overpayment of taxes corrected by lowering taxes. The illusion represented by reported profits would be maintained.

In an address, a recent chairman of the SEC, Harold M. Williams, provided another clue when he quietly noted that since executive compensation is often tied to the bottom line, it is possible that many managers are being rewarded for supposedly increasing earnings when, in fact, "they are running an operation which, in real terms, is dissipating its capital."[18] That perception suggests another important reason for procrastination on the issue by some executives.

Is it then possible that no responsible broad-based group, business or other-wise, will suggest or support meaningful measures to counter inflation by recog-nizing current costs of inventory and depreciation?

In fact, one group has come forth to play the heroic role, and it is probably the most unlikely in the country: the certified public accountants (CPAs) through the Financial Accounting Standards Board. On them falls the task of trying to stop the immolation of the capitalistic system by those who run it and by those who tax it.

Although it is not in the CPAs' repertoire, a way to cut the Gordian knot of continuing inflation with unacceptable unemployment is to increase cash flow without raising prices. Moving to universal use of LIFO and current cost depreciation will raise cash flow without higher prices or higher profits, which would magnify the next round of inflation.

I do not exclude some moderate price increases to improve return on new investment, but on the whole, higher profits will come later as new plants and equipment reduce costs and permit retirement of old, high-cost capacity. Indeed, the need to obtain profit improvement in this way would stimulate investment of an enlarged cash flow in areas yielding the highest improvements in productivity.

For LIFO management need only adopt the practice and take the probable consequences: a reduction of reported profits in the first year or two after the changeover as undercosting gives way to current costing of inventory sold. Stockholders and other outsiders can advise management as to how they feel about such a change.

The decision to propose or agree to current cost depreciation of plants and equipment rests in part with the administration but more important with Congress, which would have to revise the tax laws.

The principle involved is simple. Allow (or prescribe) year-by-year recovery of the purchasing power of plants and equipment used up or worn out, instead of only its historical cost as is done at present. This does not require recovery of replacement cost, because what is needed is not a duplication of often obsolete plants and equipment but the recovery of an amount of purchasing power with the same command over capital goods that it had when originally invested.

My point is this: the U.S. culture is governed by a DNA chain that endangers its continuation because the chain fails to signal a change in course when capital starvation saps its vitality.

Business executives deplore the economic illiteracy of the U.S. people, and particularly of educators and their students. Most of these same executives have seen the capital of their companies erode for want of adequate costing of goods sold and provision for replacement of plants and equipment used. The best program of economic education begins with business itself insisting on correcting the dissipation of its own capital and its leaders insisting that all other institutions in our society do the same. The SEC and the CPAs have given us a start by requiring disclosure of real costs and profits as well as the unreal ones that are reported. The president and Congress have yet to show by tax reform of allowable depreciation and appropriate budget policies that they have received the message.

NOTES

1. Annual Report of the Council of Economic Advisers, *Economic Report of the President* (Washington, D.C.: Government Printing Office, 1979), p. 128; idem (1980), p. 141.

2. The understatement of costs for nonfinancial corporations has been chronicled since 1965 by George Terborgh in studies for the Machinery and Allied Products Institute. See George Terborgh, *Inflation and Profits* (Washington, D.C.: Machinery and Allied Products Institute, 1980). Terborgh's data are based on Department of Commerce estimates of current costs — historical costs adjusted for inflation — of inventory and depreciation and a recalculation of profits reported to the Internal Revenue Service to reflect these inflation adjustments.

3. Failure of the relatively high savings rate of the United States to be translated into a higher growth in productivity may be accounted for in part by a rise in the proportion of capital going into housing — from 16 percent in the late 1960s to 28.5 percent by 1977.

4. The thesis just advanced depends heavily on a paper summarizing a research study for the National Council on Life Insurance given by its director. See George M. von Furstenberg, "Productivity and Development . . . Past and Prospective" (Paper presented before the International Business Economics Association, New York City, October 10, 1979).

5. These subsidies include mortgage interest deduction from personal income, mortgage guarantees, exclusion of rapidly rising capital gains on house sales from taxation if reinvested in homes, and a one-time exclusion of up to $100,000 on gains from sales of personal residences, as well as government-subsidized secondary markets for mortgages. See Anthony Downs, "Too Much Capital for Housing," *Brookings Bulletin* (Summer 1980).

6. Edward F. Denison, "Explanations of Declining Productivity Growth," *Survey of Current Business*, 59, no. 8 (August 1979): p. 3. Denison uses output per employed person as his measure of productivity, not per man-hour, nor other concepts that are used in some

other studies. Therefore, absolute numbers of derived productivity growth rates will differ among sources, depending on the concepts and measures used.

7. Ibid., pp. 3, 4.

8. A cogent analysis of these changes is included in a publication by the Work in America Institute, *The Future of Older Workers in America* (Scarsdale, N.Y.: Work in America Institute, 1980).

9. Here *CED* specifically refers to the CED's Research and Policy Committee, which is responsible for policy statements.

10. Committee for Economic Development, *Taxes and the Budget* (New York: CED, 1947).

11. Committee for Economic Development, *Growth and Taxes* (New York: CED, 1961).

12. Committee for Economic Development, *Stimulating Technological Progress* (New York: CED, 1980).

13. See Committee for Economic Development, *Capital Needs of the United States: the Next Decade* (New York: Columbia University Press, 1977).

14. Committee for Economic Development, *Reducing Tax Rates for Production and Growth* (New York: CED, 1962).

15. There is one basis for a tax credit or exemption for dividends received that is thoroughly consistent with the passed-on view of the corporate profits tax. When a company can be shown to have paid dividends out of capital (for example, through failure to use LIFO or current cost depreciation), the stockholder should be exempt from tax on such dividends, as, in effect, they are a return on his capital. As noted in Table 4, this would have called for a tax credit to stockholders possibly totaling $9.2 billion in 1974, the amount paid out in dividends in excess of real profits after taxes.

16. The amount of undercosting reflected in the Commerce Department's inventory valuation adjustment for business as a whole was $52 billion in 1979 and was running at a $36 billion annual rate in the first three quarters of 1980.

17. *Business Week*, September 8, 1980, p. 34.

18. Reported in the *New York Times*, December 14, 1977.

5

THE SOCIAL RESPONSIBILITIES
OF LARGE COMPANIES

A perennial subject of discussion by the executives of large companies is the application of antitrust laws to the problem of company bigness. On one occasion when an executive made a plea for study of this subject by the combined group of executives and academic advisers — a plea that threatened to stampede the group into an affirmative conclusion — an adviser and sometime president of the American Economic Association made a telling observation that survived and was quoted for several years.

As I look around this room, I cannot identify an executive of a company that has not either been the subject of an antitrust suit or a consent decree or is not faced with one or the other. Your names will all appear on this study as being responsible for it. You can and may very well produce a study that is the epitome of reasonabless. Even if you do that, it will be a waste of time. Nobody will believe you.

Before the end of the 1960s, however, a combination of social problems facing the country was brought so forcibly to the attention of executives that the subject of the responsibility of big business to society and vice versa created an irresistible interest. Youth in colleges and universities had begun to turn against all elements of the establishment, including their own collegiate institutions. Riots had broken out among the minority populations of large cities as a reaction against substandard housing, lack of employment opportunities, racial discrimination of all kinds, and an explosive atmosphere precipitated by the assassination of Martin Luther King, Jr.

In this climate, business executives began to feel an overwhelming obligation to appraise their own role in dealing with long-smoldering problems that governments and other institutions had been left to handle and had handled ineffectively. Those executives who harbored a desire to say something in favor of the benignity of big business united with those who wanted business to assume large responsibility for curing social ills of all kinds. They questioned whether the structure of business, restrained as it was by the antitrust laws, could be expected to conform to the public's demands that it become more involved in social problems. This mood brought about not only a five-year study[2] of the social responsibility of business but a succession of projects on the welfare system, health care, education for the disadvantaged, and especially jobs for the disadvantaged.

In studying the social obligations of business and its capability to carry them out, the participants discovered a gulf between the main body of economics and economists, on the one hand, and the conception of enlightened self-interest, as perceived by business executives, on the other. Their studies and discussions produced a wealth of case material on how far apart were the preconceptions of academics and business leaders in their approach to the involvement of business in social problems and to the way in which the business role is defined (or not defined) in this critical area. The task was summed up at the conclusion of the study by one of its leaders. The study, he said, provides a perspective that a great many business and management people, public servants, and legislators are looking for. It is a perspective that moves between two extremes — the extreme that attempts to persuade people that the only function of business is to produce maximum profits (an extreme, he contended, that no one seriously pursued today) and the other extreme that all the ills of U.S. society are the responsibility of business and largely a result of its behavior.

PERCEPTIONS AND GOALS OF CORPORATE BUSINESS

The committee charged with making the study on social responsibilities of business began quite logically with some general considerations of the nature of business and the goals that the business firm seeks to attain. Early in the discussions, a top executive of a company manufacturing office products threw down a gauntlet that was to occupy the group for a considerable period and that, in fact, was never fully disposed of. He said that we have listened to some views dating back to Adam Smith: let business alone. Let it be governed by greed. The more greed, the better. Businesses will fight one another; their competition will straighten things out. That idea, he said, is as dead as a doornail. If we intend to get out a paper that is going to satisfy the majority of economists, I think it won't be worth a damn.

An executive of another large manufacturing corporation, who throughout the discussions served as an elder statesman in resolving conflicting views, suggested that a good working definition of the *fundamental goal* of corporations is to serve the objectives of the society of which they are a part. On that basis, he said, you can take into consideration the profit motive as a constructive means of attaining society's objectives, or even the capacity of the profit and price system [as compared with other systems] for satisfying the fundamental aspirations of different societies.

It became increasingly clear as the discussion proceeded that the participants held widely diverse conceptions on which they based their remarks about business and the economic system. Despite the contention of a retailing executive that to do so would polarize small and large businesses, the group decided that its principal focus would be on the large, publicly owned corporate enterprises, which constitute the dominant group in our business system. The large corporate enterprise thus became the major focus of attention.

An executive whose background had originally been law made a succinct statement that separated large corporations from small firms. The corporation, he said, is the fundamental basis for the type of business that we are discussing because it receives a charter which provides limited liability, perpetuity, succession of ownership, and a pool of resources under a succession of managements. The corporate form creates powers and capabilities which are quite different in kind, and in effect on society, from those of a personal, private business. From that basic point it is fair to argue that the corporate form, being a privilege extended by law and not a right which is inherent in any individual, is recognized by society as an institution from which flow special obligations. The "statesman executive" (who will henceforth be so identified) added his own interpretation to this judgment by observing that if an individual is running a business of his own, his only objective in life is to maximize his own personal fortune; this leads to the application of criteria and motivations quite different from those of corporate businesses. The basic objective of the large, publicly owned, professionally managed corporation must be to keep itself healthy and growing and to perpetuate itself indefinitely. It is these basic propositions that distinguish the conception of business, as held by most executives of large companies, from the atomistic, almost mindless profit-maximizing concept of the business firm that is inherent in the laissez-faire approach.

As the group seemed to coalesce around these distinctions, an adviser who was one of the country's leading political theorists was led to suggest that the large, corporate, publicly owned and professionally managed enterprise was in many ways analogous to a unit of government. In a confidential memorandum for the author, he later wrote that in his view when a group of men banded themselves together and were sanctioned by society to perform a generally needed function for others through a large corporation, and that corporation is able to exempt itself in large measure from the market mechanism and has the power to carry out its decisions, it becomes a "political institution." Such an organization is in a position to determine in considerable measure what it will charge its customers, what it will pay its suppliers and workers, to whom it will shift taxes levied upon it, and what kind of service it will give now and in the future. It is a "sovereign body," which can decide for itself how much of the

GNP it will take for itself. No such sovereign group, he argued, can exist within a society except by consent of that society. When that sanction is extended in fact or by law, the corporation becomes a piece of government.

He continued to the logical conclusion, following from the premises he set forth, that the exercise of such power is sanctioned by a society not for the benefit of the corporate group but because of the benefits that this extraordinary authority confers on society. This benefit is therefore to be determined by society — that is, ultimately by the political process. By this logic, large modern corporations, particularly those dealing with manufacturing, resource extraction, power, transportation, communications, and finance, are political institutions.

While the political theorist may have overstated his argument, he did a great deal to clarify the thinking that became the basis for many of the arguments for the exercise of social responsibility by large companies. Every large company must be managed with a view to what in political theory would be considered its constituencies: other companies (including competitors), those who work for the company, its stockholders, its customers, and the various governments that regulate and tax it, not to mention the public at large.

THE ROLE OF PROFITS

If the structure of the large business corporation and of its constituencies is properly defined in the preceding statements, then the role of profits in the business system as we know it must undergo a considerable amount of rethinking. This the committee undertook to do over a period of several years.

An early statement, which turned out in the end to be one of the most truthful, was made by the statesman executive referred to earlier. He said that perhaps we ought to start on a very fundamental level and define the objectives of any form of economic organization in terms of the total national well-being. Business should justify itself in terms of its total contribution to society, just as education, medicine, or any other sector must do. A special problem of the public posture of business is the general belief that it exists to make profits, that profits represent a selfish goal, and that business people in pursuing profits seek to take something away from other people. In his view, business does not exist just to make profits. Profits, instead, are a natural concomitant of the growth and development of business over time but are incidental to the total contribution of a business to society.

In making this statement the executive was relying upon the principle that some parts of society produce a surplus, which enables other parts of society to exist and flourish. In other words, he argued that some types of economic activity are more productive than others, a view contrary to most of modern economics but common among executives of large companies. It is from this notion that a principle was formulated stating that any organization should be judged by its contribution to society but that on balance business would be found to have an overwhelming surplus to contribute to the rest of society. Whether sustainable or not, that view did a lot for the morale of the executives.

Most executives disputed the notion that business should maximize its profits. Instead, and in keeping with the political analogy, the executive organization of a company should be considered as situated in what could be compared with the hub of a wheel. The spokes represent the desires and interests of various constituents: customers, employees, stockholders, and others. The customers want lower prices, the employees want higher wages or more benefits, stockholders want either higher dividends or higher capital appreciation, and the government always wants more taxes. Cheating one constituency for the benefit of another may produce strains that cause the whole structure to fall apart. The company has to develop a management rationale that produces continuing growth so that it can demonstrably meet the conflicting interests with which it must contend.

This view was challenged not just by economists but by other executives. Everybody, said one executive who spoke for many, should tend to his own shop and do the best job he can toward producing the maximum for the lowest cost for the widest distribution. Meeting that standard, he argued, is what constitutes a good job by a corporate officer. If he does that job well, he is performing his social obligation.

Another added that he thought the trouble with most of his business colleagues was that they were afraid to admit that they were in business principally to make profits. He laid it down as an axiom that no company exists unless its main and principal goal is to make a profit in a legitimate manner. The chairman asked whether a corporation should absolutely exclude every consideration except that which specifically and fundamentally lends itself to the purpose of making a profit. A Wall Street executive responded by saying that profit is important because profit becomes the measure of the value of the economic service provided to society. This immediately led to a considerable excursion, too lengthy to be included here, the gist of which was that profits are essential as a means to an end; they are not an end in themselves, although essential for the continuity and growth of the firm.

But do profits measure either social or economic performance? A sociologist made the most telling answer by pointing out that capital investment in the labor force of a company, in its customer relations, in its community relations, and in other areas constitutes a far larger investment than is shown by the figures on its balance sheet that represent its net worth. This unrecorded capital could be converted into reported profits for a period of time but only at the expense of the long-run profitability and growth of the company. An executive of a large, highly profitable firm agreed, adding that simply by changing allocations to research, or market development, or replacement of capital, or a number of other optional areas of expense, profits in the short run can be appreciably increased for some time. The level of profits is therefore not a good measure of social contribution, at least in the short run.

An economist pointed out another and probably the greatest flaw of profit as a measure of social performance: Profits depend to a large extent on the market power of the corporation. Companies with considerable market power can control their profits with much more facility than those with little market power. Later, I shall consider this subject at length.

One of the most enlightening arguments against short-term profit maximizing was made by an executive who continually stressed the need for large companies to make themselves attractive to bright young people. We have, he said, a lot of junior executives. How long are we going to lead them if our policy is to make the utmost profit as soon as possible? He thought that many of us fail to understand that no business is any greater than the human beings in it. And whether we like it or not, the human being has a moral side, a public interest side, and you cannot lead youngsters and develop a strong management team that will keep your company viable unless you lead them with something more than the maximum amount of profit that you can make. Are businessmen scared, he asked, or really ashamed of being motivated by what is right – by conscience? Unless the management of his company, he said, had the instinct to be fair, right, and decent, we would fall apart. There is within every one of us the instinct of what is moral – what is the right and fair thing to do. Why in blazes have we drawn this cloak of Adam Smith around us so tightly? Are we afraid to be caught naked without it? What are we afraid of? We have got to have guts to admit that we are men.

A decade later, in a published symposium, Fletcher Byrom, chairman of the Koppers Company, illustrated the same point by relating a question to and response from a group of his own company's managers.

> Assuming that the material benefits would be the same regardless of what kind of a job you had, would you opt for the job you have in the Koppers Company? . . . There were twenty people and eighteen of them said no. I was absolutely flabbergasted. Everybody in the group recognized that Adam Smith was right when he said that the greed of the individual eventually resulted in benefit to the whole. However, they said they had a twinge of conscience down "deep in their gut," that told them that they would rather *not* be working for a profit making institution. . . . They didn't understand the mission of a company like the Koppers Company in our economic system. They really thought that if they could work full time as a head of [some nonprofit-making organization] they would be making a more significant contribution to the well-being of society than they were as effective managers in the Koppers Company.[3]

An economist-methodologist finally put the matter in broadest perspective by observing that economists are using, or ought to be using, a profit-maximizing model as a scientific device to explain behavior. He observed that they frequently move from the profit-maximizing model as an explanatory device to the conclusion that if reality is not like the explanatory device, we should try to modify the reality to make it like the model, which assumes a corporation to have an obligation to be a profit-maximizing organization. Obviously, he said, this is moving away from the use of the model as a scientific device, since it cannot be demonstrated that pursuit of a profit-maximizing objective would contribute any more to the welfare of society, or to the productivity of the business community, than would some other model.

An industrial executive took much the same point of view in a letter to another. He argued that the facts of modern industrial organization had outstripped traditional theory. Some scholars meet this divergence, he observed, by advocating changes in industrial organization so that fact and theory agree. Others, realizing that this approach logically requires breaking up the industrial complex, but recognizing that this is both impractical and self-defeating, end with a bagful of illogical and ineffective proposals. Too few scholars, he concluded, are at work analyzing the realities of the modern industrial economy with a view to evolving new fundamentals of economic theory compatible with what actually goes on in the world.

The executive statesman summed up the state of knowledge very well by saying that if business is to use profit as a guide — and we believe that it must — we also should take a look at what kind of profitability measures business is using. The concept of profitability that has been used by business is not consistent with the kind of job that must now be done by corporations to accomplish social objectives as we perceive them. (This subject has been discussed in part in Chapter 4.)

CHOICE OF GOALS BY MANAGEMENT

In discussions of the role of the large corporation in meeting the needs of society outside the marketplace as well as within it, the interest of stockholders cannot be overlooked and, in fact, might be crucial. One banking executive expressed himself unequivocally on this as preparation of the final paper neared its end. I think, he said, that we have sold the stockholders short in this paper. I think that we do not reflect enough confidence in stockholders, who also are Americans and who, if properly approached, will approve those social purposes which the company thinks it should adopt. Another executive responded with the observation that more than half of his own company's stock was held by institutions of various kinds. He was impressed by the comments of several institutional investors that their businesses were not managing businesses but managing money. If, he said, they don't like the way we run our company, they are going to liquidate their holdings in it and move into something else. They don't have a great deal of interest, it seems, in disciplining management with respect to the company's social actions.

The statesman executive in an earlier discussion had supplied a more detailed rationale of the relationship of management to stockholders. Theoretically, he said, the stockholders chose management, and theoretically management runs the business in the interest of the stockholders. Actually, he continued, I don't think that statement is true. There are different forms of capital; for example, common stock in the hands of the investor is a form of liquid capital. If a stockholder doesn't like the way a company is being run, except in extreme cases he will sell his stock and invest in some company that is run more to his liking. So the stockholders don't really exert too much effect on management, but they do choose to invest in companies that are run the way they prefer. Knowing this, management to a certain extent can almost choose its own stockholders by pursuing its own corporate goals. He cited one company that was financially strong but followed the policy of making a relatively low payout of earnings in dividends — only about a third. As a result, the company's stock was held mainly by investors who preferred stability of earnings and growth to higher current dividends.

SOCIALLY RESPONSIBLE MANAGEMENT AND THE INTEREST OF STOCKHOLDERS

Stimulated by such discussions, two economists prepared a classic rationale reconciling the socially responsible actions of corporations with the interests of stockholders.[4] The classic case against socially responsible expenditure or investment by one company in amounts beyond what the company can get back with a competitive rate of profit is that other firms, or society itself, realize the benefits rather than that company. However, if socially responsible expenditures or investments made by a firm yield benefits that can be realized by other firms, the case can be made that stockholders generally benefit from the socially responsible expenditure or investment of even a single firm. Because typical stockholders have diversified portfolios (more than two-thirds of listed stocks are in the hands of institutions), the gains of other firms offset the cost of the socially responsible action of the firm undertaking socially responsible expenditures. After a careful theoretical analysis of a variety of possible cases, the authors state:

> The conclusion of this analysis is that the proposition that corporate involvement in social policy is contrary to the stockholders' interest is both misleading and irrelevant. Involvement in social policy is tantamount to the adoption of a policy of evaluating investment opportunities including returns other than those directly accruing to the investing corporation in the form in increased profits. . . . The adoption of a policy of including all returns appropriable through the market system will enable [diversified] investors to reach higher welfare levels than they would if corporations adhered to a narrower approach to evaluation of returns.[5]

The foregoing conclusion applies to voluntary, socially responsible actions of corporations. The results postulated can be better ensured if governments make appropriate rules that exclude the possibility of mavericks' receiving appropriable benefits without any investment or expenditure of their own.

PRIMARY GOAL OF THE LARGE CORPORATION

If maximizing profit is not the be-all and end-all of corporate behavior, and if an intricate and complicated set of socially responsible actions is not only desirable in terms of the welfare of the corporation but also in terms of stockholders in general, what goal is the large corporation seeking? For operating companies, as opposed to investment companies, the answer from both executives and academics was unequivocal: The primary goal is perpetuation of the institution, keeping the company growing and a viable part of the country. This goal the behavioral scientists translated into ecological terms: the prime essence of ecology is to ensure viability and growth. But in taking that view, corporations must be in business to make a profit because profits are indispensable to remaining viable, to remaining alive. Beyond remaining alive, the executives stressed the need for growth, as has been noted earlier. A company must have growth because that is the only way it can perpetuate itself as an institution. It must attract outstanding young people to have a strong management organization. To do that it must be able to provide increased opportunities for individual growth and development through growth of the company.

To this line of reasoning the executive of one of the largest transnational companies provided a global dimension. It is not just the growth of your own company compared with its past that is important; it is also how your company is doing against your competitors and equally how this country is doing compared with others; how well are we standing up in creating wealth which can then be distributed so as to serve the needs of our society? The statesman executive added, When you identify the basic objectives of the large corporation with fundamentally sound and absolutely parallel national objectives, you build greater respect.

To avoid any misinterpretation of the foregoing discussion, I will summarize it in my own way. The profit-maximizing, almost mindless, concept of the firm used by economists and the widely divergent view of many executives of large companies result mainly from a difference in perspectives. Economists think of firms as being so numerous and small that they need not take the external consequences of their actions into account; hence, they use a profit-maximizing rule. Executives of large companies know that what they do affects constituencies outside the firm and even outside the country. They must take such constituencies into account. Their primary goals must be survival and growth, both of which would be jeopardized by mindless profit maximizing. If, as will be demonstrated later, large companies dominate the economy, the second view must be the working basis for policy making.

CORPORATE DECISIONS FOR SOCIAL ACTION: EXECUTIVES VERSUS ACADEMICS

The chief executive of a manufacturing company was reminiscing about how decisions on social issues were made in his company.

When we all recognize that we are human beings and talk with other people on that basis, even in discussions with the board of directors, we get the kind of leadership that we want. I have had a lot of amusing experiences with my own board over the years. When I became an executive, the company had a very conservative board. It was only because I made that company grow that I survived. As a youngster I used to give long rationalizations for doing something that needed to be done in the humanitarian area. If I wanted to put in a profit-sharing plan or group life insurance, I could certainly rationalize and I would write pages, then support my proposal with figures. Early in my career the reaction of the board was that they liked the proposal because they were human, too, but what was it going to cost? "Come up with the facts and figures and prove that it coincides with the profit motive," they said. After I did that everybody was relieved, somebody moved to accept the proposal, and we put it into practice. But it finally got to the point where I would say, "I have a feeling that we ought to do so and so here and now. Will you take it on? Do you want a rationalization − I have one right here and I will give it to you," and they got into the habit of responding, "If you think it's the right thing to do, go ahead."

How far should the corporation go in the social action arena? How much should it depart from its normal profit and loss calculations when it undertakes socially responsible actions that may not yield the normal rate of return or may not even yield any measurable profit at all? On this question most of the academic advisers who were economists felt very much at home and arrived at virtual unanimity. I will cite a few of their opinions.

Said one of the older and most experienced among them: I suppose that the major issue is, Who should supply the rules of the road which would provide that those ostensibly seeking profits also should be making economic choices to advance the quality of life? Said he, There is a school of thought that argues this is not the job of the chief executive of a corporation but the job of Washington, D.C.; it isn't your function; you [executives] must live by the rules rather than formulate them.

Another argued: On the matter of what is in the national interest, on the one side is a government decision and on the other is a business decision and these two things should not be mixed. The appropriate incentive in this area is a question for the government to decide.

A third argued that he grew exceedingly nervous about the idea of having individual groups, on their own, make decisions about what is good for society.

Most of us, he said, tend to forget the last couple of sentences with which Adam Smith ended the passage on the invisible hand: I have never known much good done by those who affected to trade for the public good. It is an affectation, indeed, not very common among merchants, and very few words need be employed in dissuading them from it. If we make it profitable for businessmen to do what society feels they ought to do, we unleash the great, unnoticed power and efficiency of the business community and enable and encourage business to do those things on a scale which really promises to be effective.

Another economist: My own feeling on such questions is that it would be better if the corporations as such avoided taking the position that one of their functions is to help formulate social goals. I think social goals should be formulated by the citizens of the United States. And while the corporation is an artificial citizen, it isn't quite that kind of citizen.

An executive of a business advisory service attempted to build a bridge: Anything that you can do to build better theoretical background and understanding of good citizenship in business I applaud, but you never tap either the financial or dynamic resources of business so long as you ask business to do something from the standpoint of good citizenship. The only way to do that is to play the market forces because that is what business is all about. Businesses could do a great deal in the social action arena if the rules of the game were restructured to encourage them.

Another economist came up with the time-honored tool of his trade: "If the government were to levy specific taxes, it might push business firms into finding it in their own interest to conform to a socially responsible standard and a very important public purpose would have been served. But it will not be served by one business trying to live up to the standard and thereby taxing its own stockholders while its competitors do not. No business can force its competitors to follow its lead in social action."

The statesman executive forgot his role at this point, interjecting that he disagreed with the foregoing statement just as thoroughly as the economist disagreed with business autonomy in social action decisions. He added that governments are seldom able to formulate any kind of policy that has a specific end in mind and were seldom consistent in continuing a tax policy without modifying it in a variety of ways, which tended to ruin its effectiveness.

THREE SCHOOLS ON SOCIAL RESPONSIBILITY

The preceding citation of their views demonstrates that many of the economic and other advisers obviously were not satisfied with the prescriptions by corporate executives on social policy. One school of economists sums up its philosophy by stating flatly that the social responsibility of business is to increase profits. (The rejection of that view by most participating executives is self-evident.)

A second school, which might be called that of enlightened self-interest, stresses that, far from having a single goal — for example, profits or even growth — the large corporation has many goals. While all of these are interrelated with the primary ecological goal, which is to stay alive and grow, these goals are attainable only by the pursuit of such objectives as cultivating markets for the firm's products; employing, training, motivating, and providing a high quality of work life and a high standard of living to employees; giving stockholders a reasonable rate of return sufficient to bolster the firm's need for additional capital from time to time; helping to create and maintain healthy communities in which the firm's operations are located and its employees live; maintaining good and cooperative relationships with the various governments that regulate, control, and tax the firm; and pursuing many other objectives that in the end will improve the quality of life not only of those associated with the company but of people in the country as a whole. Pursuit of all these goals is in the long run self-interest of the company. Management must discover how to balance the interests and the outcomes of the decisions it makes and the actions it takes.

A third school, noted above, distrusts the corporation's own decision-making process in pursuing goals other than profitability but favors socially responsible action. The considerable amount of discussion by its adherents can be summed up in the concept that it is the role of government to establish the framework and set the rules that companies should follow in pursuit of their social responsibilities.

There was no real controversy over the pursuit of objectives that are required by law or regulation. Almost everyone opted for conformity with duly authorized rules of this kind. These included conforming to the requirement of equal employment opportunity, health and safety regulations, pollution control, and the like. Similarly, not a great deal of heat was generated by the argument that if the government is willing to contract for services, the company should go the route of social responsibility to whatever extent it could. For example, government-financed education and training programs of business got high marks, and numerous cases were cited in which the company was operating in some labor markets where there was no choice but to upgrade the disadvantaged in order to obtain an adequate supply of employees. In fact, recent surveys have uncovered a far wider business participation in government-financed employment training programs than was known to most business people or the public.

CORPORATE LEADERSHIP IN SOCIAL PROGRAMS

Controversy grew, however, over the role of companies and their executives in promoting social programs that were perceived to be needed but that are not required by government. Some executives argued that an individual company should undertake voluntarily and on its own as much of such programs as it considers to be in its own interest, especially if such participation results in a fallout that is good for corporate business as a whole. As we shall see, there is a considerable amount of such activity. If it is impractical for a single company to do very much on its own, it may be possible for a consortium or trade association, or some other logical grouping of companies, to undertake a program that benefits all of them. A classic example is the Keep America Beautiful program, which has as its objective cleaning up roadsides and public places littered by bottles, cans, and other residues of product consumption.

The real controversy arises when it is impractical for a company to follow either the route of individual voluntarism or of joining a consortium having similar interests. If a social program requires government incentives, compulsion, or regulation to be effective, what should be the role of the company in encouraging such programs? Members of the group cited pollution as an example. To the knowledge of those involved, at least two federal government departments came to a group of company executives before federal legislation was enacted and requested them to give advice on the framing of appropriate governmental actions for dealing with pollution problems. Both the Department of Health, Education and Welfare and the Department of Commerce requested such assistance, and neither received any positive response from the groups approached. Representatives of the Department of Commerce laid their cards on the table, revealing that within two years of the time of this request legislation to control water and air pollution would be introduced in Congress. The federal government did not have the competence to draft legislation that would be adequate or acceptable but felt that the know-how for the kind of control that would be acceptable and effective lay within the corporate sector and no other place. Even though it might look as though they were asking the chickens to join the fox for mutual benefit, government representatives were willing to take the risk in the interest of sound legislation.

The record of industry in opposing the antipollution legislation that was finally drafted, and the difficulties they had in living with it are well known. Some executives who went through this frustrating experience vowed not to let it happen again and went to work on other social problems not yet cast into concrete legislation. Groups of company executives have come up with some first-rate proposals for dealing with reform of the welfare system (a movement that is still going on) and for instituting a health care system that would retain the best parts of the present system. One group even went so far as to make proposals — which were in large measure accepted — for improving the financing of higher education in ways that would preserve the private colleges and provide greater choice for students.

Oddly enough, other than to support civil rights legislation, there were very few instances in which executives took a firm stand on optional matters having to do with equality of rights. The most notable case was open housing. One top executive insisted that he should have the civil right as a citizen to go on local television and radio in his home city in support of open housing. He felt that being the head of his company should not deprive him of the right to express himself on such an issue. Another executive said that he took a strong public position in favor of open housing in his headquarters community but that, unlike his colleague, he did it as a representative of his company. His company had found it impossible to hire really good black college graduates because when they came to town they would be forced to live in undesirable places. His support of open housing, he felt, was in the self-interest of his company and he did not dissociate himself from it.

A CHAIRMAN'S SUMMARY

The then-chairman of the CED, William C. Stolk, entered the discussion at a number of points but once in the process decided to unburden himself in a public address that provided a useful synthesis of the major thrust of the committee:

> There is almost no social task to which all corporations could not make a significant contribution. This is because our corporations have unique capabilities in research, technology, and managerial skills, and these are precisely what is needed. If Aerojet General and North American Aviation can apply systems analysis to pollution abatement and public transportation for the state of California, if Eastern Gas and Fuel Associates can build large-scale, low-rent housing in the Boston slums, every corporation ought to be able to find an area of social improvement that matches its capabilities. . . .
> Many government leaders at all levels — federal, state, and municipal — have increasingly recognized the limitations of public agencies in coping effectively with many of our social problems.

Recognizing the profitability problem that had figured prominently in the committee's discussion, he made two suggestions for dealing with it. First, the corporation must be clear about what is required to do the job, including tax benefits, specific types of government assistance, and other such inducements. If the government is insensitive to such requirements, business should make a concerted effort to interest government in the problem. The appropriate public authorities could then determine whether the results would be worth the cost, in light of alternative ways of getting the job done. Second,

> is to re-examine our traditional concepts and measurements of profit. . . . We capitalize the buildings and machinery that we use, but the crucial human assets of the corporation are not inventoried as carefully as the wood supplies, aren't managed with the same kind of cause-effect concern as is applied to the manufacturing process, and don't show up on the balance sheet at all — even though the human assets obviously represent a higher value than all the physical assets.

Once we've placed the proper value on the human assets of the business and their contribution to profitability, we can look at training and education programs for hard-core unemployables and corporate aid to education in general as an *investment* rather than philanthropy.

He concluded by saying:

I think it is obvious that business and government must develop the same kind of effective partnership in social problem-solving that has been achieved in wartime. . . . We must insist that government . . . develop an effective organizational structure out of the present hodge-podge of agencies, define its areas of greatest competence, and also measure its results.[6]

A NOTE ON PHILANTHROPY AND SELF-INTEREST

Many may question why corporate executives in discussing the social responsibility of business spent so little time on philanthropy as such — corporate giving. Economists who stress profits as the only legitimate goal of business logically oppose philanthropy by business, and it was against the tide of these views and the legalistic argument that corporate donations were at the expense of stockholders that the pioneers in corporate philanthropy had to move. But as companies had long ago won sanction for corporate giving from the courts, Congress, and the Internal Revenue Service, one might expect that manifestion of corporate social responsibility would be heavily channeled into donations. Probably the contrary view would be more descriptive of practice, as the preceding account should indicate. Despite an allowance of 5 percent tax deductible, corporate contributions account for only about 1 percent of pretax corporate net income and about 5 percent of contributions from all sources.[7] Most corporate leaders would be the first to argue that this is no measure of their social responsibility.

While most executives of large companies stoutly argue that being socially responsible is in the long-run self-interest of the company and corporate business, this does not answer the question of whether a "good cause" should be supported. Corporate gifts must meet so far as possible the same tests of enlightened self-interest as other social action decisions. Recipients of donations, and the independent sector, generally prefer to believe that true philanthropy should be motivated by love of mankind — the original meaning of *philanthropy* — not *self-interest*, however defined. With some reason, corporate donors look askance at actions or studies by gift-supported institutions that impugn or attack corporate sacred cows or special interests. Some companies in considering contributions weigh whether a research or education group has, in the prior year or two, on balance conducted activities favorable to the company's or to corporate interests. There are some leading business executives who have advocated such a standard even for contributions to colleges and universities. Some also question whether corporate support of some good causes (even those favorable to business) may not in fact represent the substitution of the executive's values for those of the community or society.

The type of schizophrenia implied in the foregoing helps explain why philanthropy is but a small part of the corporate expression of social responsibility and why it does not account for a large part of the national total of individual and institutional giving.

It is probably a safe conclusion that top management's perceptions of the need for specific types of socially responsible corporate expenditures or investments depend on management's own conception of the company's enlightened self-interest. But what that self-interest may be depends very much on individual situations, which vary markedly from industry to industry and from case to case. When a major social problem confronts a large part of the corporate community, some common approach, such as that of the Urban Coalition, or even a common demand on government, might be expected. Reform of the welfare and health care systems might meet the test required for a common demand on government. But the corporate response to social programs is likely to be individualistic and antagonistic to joint action or to government direction. This thesis is tested in the survey summarized in the following section.

REPORTING ON THE SOCIALLY RESPONSIBLE BEHAVIOR OF BUSINESS

The foregoing account of discussions among business executives in small leadership groups faithfully reflects a widespread view that business decisions should be influenced by the expectations of business constituencies, including the general public. Polls indicate that as many as three-quarters of the business executives queried agree that the impact on society must be an important factor in all business decisions. Moreover, nearly half disagree with the proposition that business can help best by sticking to the primary objective of profit making.

Emboldened by such information, Secretary of Commerce Juanita M. Kreps proposed that the Department of Commerce develop and publish a social performance index that would "give business a way of appraising the social effects of its business operations. Businesses can use this index to provide data on environmental controls, affirmative action, minority purchasing, consumer complaint resolution, and product testing."[8]

This initiative, however desirable its intent, represents a classic case of government moving too soon, too fast, and, probably, counterproductively. Despite its intent of giving recognition to socially responsible business actions, the index, apparently, was coolly received by business and not pursued.

The views of business leaders discussed earlier in this chapter provide ample reason for this reaction. Companies face different conditions to which their executives react in their own individual ways. Their vehement arguments for exercising social responsibility are linked to insistence that courses of action be left largely to executive discretion.

At the suggestion of the author, two researchers with long experience in the field conducted a survey of business social action programs.[9] This study modestly suggests steps that each company might wisely take toward producing a social report fashioned to the company's own needs. The desirability of following this procedure in contrast to one requiring a uniform report for all companies is apparent and was clearly revealed in responses to the survey. Some service companies − for example, consultants − saw themselves being little concerned with pollution, urban renewal, or conservation. Other companies, like utilities, expressed major concern about these same areas. Social reports by the two types of firms would understandably be quite different in content and emphasis but would overlap in such areas as education, the arts, and fair employment.

We can hope that a multitude of efforts over the years to make social reports would lead to the development of something like the common law in which consistency of cases would establish norms for certain types of social performance that might be followed by most large companies, and that common norms for other types of performance might be developed on an industry-by-industry basis by companies facing similar problems.

The conclusion just cited was derived from 284 returned questionnaires in the Corson-Steiner study. The study validated the premise, so frequently argued by the executives who participated in the discussions, that "large publicly owned, professionally managed companies" were indeed concerned about social responsibility and were likely to be working on a social audit, or expecting that one would be required in the future.

But firms pursued different routes toward social responsibility. Of those reporting, the 10 most important socially responsible programs being pursued (of 58 listed) are shown in Table 7.

Presumably companies pursue different programs because they face different problems. Moreover, the 58 programs listed in the questionnaire did not even include many that some companies found to be important. Companies showed the same diversity and independent initiatives that the committee discussions had revealed.

Moreover, directly relevant to the question of a government index of social performance were the replies to a question about obstacles confronted by companies that were attempting to make social (audit) performance reports. (See Table 8.)

For the reasons cited, and others, most (53 percent) of the companies that make social performance reports confine their distribution to executives or directors or both.

TABLE 7
Ten Leading Social and Economic Programs for Which Companies Have Made Significant Commitments of Money and/or Personnel

Rank	Program	Number of Companies
1	Employment and advancement opportunities for minorities	244
2	Direct financial aid to schools, including scholarships, grants, tuition refunds	238
3	Active recruitment of the disadvantaged	199
4	Improvement of work/career opportunities	191
5	Installation of modern pollution abatement equipment	189
6	Increasing productivity in the private sector of the economy	180
7	Direct financial support to art institutions and the performing arts	177
8	Facilitating equality of results by continued training and other special programs (for minorities and women)	176
9	Improving the innovativeness and performance of business management	174
10	Engineering new facilities for minimum (adverse) environmental effects	169

Source: Adapted from John J. Corson and George A. Steiner, *Measuring Business's Social Performance: The Corporate Social Audit* (New York: Committee for Economic Development, 1974), pp. 27-29.

TABLE 8
Obstacles to Social Performance Reporting
(in percent)

Rank	Obstacle	Order of Importance				
		1	2	3	4	5
1	Inability to develop measures of performance that everyone will accept	98	57	29	8	4
2	Inability to make credible cost/benefit analysis to guide company actions	58	63	25	32	8
3	Inability to develop consensus as to what activities shall be covered	38	35	50	34	8
4	Inability to develop consensus on ways to organize information	15	29	43	41	22
5	Danger to the company in publishing the results of social audits	8	18	15	14	66

Source: Adapted from John J. Corson and George A. Steiner, *Measuring Business's Social Performance: The Corporate Social Audit* (New York: Committee for Economic Development, 1974), p. 36.

The results of the survey show clearly that social responsibility has high priority in large companies. Three-quarters of the 254 companies responding on the question make social performance reports, and all those having sales of $10 billion or more make them. That these reports are mostly for internal use by business policy makers does not derogate from their importance; indeed, their limited circulation emphasizes the probability that they are taken seriously. The existence and internal use of such reports at highest company levels confirm that as a guide to company policy social performance reporting is of significant importance in the United States.

Social performance reporting or social audits are also of great concern to European businesses and their constituencies, particularly labor organizations. While reporting is still voluntary, except in France, there is extensive experimentation going on in larger firms of industrial countries. In France a social report devoted exclusively to employment conditions was required by law in 1976 from the larger firms.[10] In the United States, stagflation has diminished concern about the social performance of business, but it is clearly a subject that will be of growing importance, as will the contributions of large companies to the making of national social policies.

NOTES

1. Committee for Economic Development, *The Social Responsibilities of Business Corporations* (New York: CED, 1971).

2. This argument was later published by Rensis Likert for the CED. See Rensis Likert, "The Influence of Social Research on Corporate Responsibility," in *A New Rationale for Corporate Social Policy*, Committee for Economic Development Supplementary Paper no. 31 (New York: CED, 1970).

3. George A. Steiner, ed., *Business and Its Changing Environment*, Proceedings of a Conference at the University of California-Los Angeles, July 24-August 3, 1977 (Los Angeles: Graduate School of Management, University of California-Los Angeles, April 1968), pp. 116-17.

4. Henry C. Wallich and John J. MacGowan, *Stockholder Interest and the Corporation's Role in Social Policy*, in *A New Rationale for Corporate Social Policy*, CED Supplementary Paper no. 31 (New York: CED, 1970).

5. Ibid., p. 55.

6. William C. Stolk, "Beyond Profitability — Defining Corporate Goals." Mimeographed. (Address to National Association of Business Economists, New York, September 26, 1968).

7. American Association of Fund-Raising Counsel, *Giving USA*, 1979 Annual Report (New York: American Association of Fund Raising Counsel, 1980)

8. Press Release, U.S., Department of Commerce, *Commerce News*, October 19, 1977.

9. John J. Corson and George A. Steiner, *Measuring Business's Social Performance: The Corporate Social Audit* (New York: Committee for Economic Development, 1974).

10. The report calls for information covering the last three years on employment, wages and fringe benefits, health and safety and other working conditions, training, industrial relations, and company welfare expenditures.

6

IDEOLOGICAL CONFLICT OVER
THE POWER OF UNIONS

When the thaw in U.S.-Soviet relations got under way in the late 1950s, one contribution to it was a private dinner (January 15, 1959) for Anastas Mikoyan, first deputy premier of the Soviet Union, given by the Committee for Economic Development (CED) chairman Donald K. David and his executive committee. The conversation was entirely off the record, but a comment by the guest of honor reveals a grave misapprehension on his part, and the response to it provides insight into the state of mind of his U.S. hosts, almost all of whom were corporate executives and directors.[1]

Mikoyan expanded warmly on the prospect that since businessmen did not agree with many of the policies of the U.S. government toward the Soviet Union and since, as the most important power in the United States, they were in a position to control their government, U.S. government policies toward the Soviet Union could be expected to change.

This attribution of power created such a chorus of disagreement among the U.S. executives present that Mikoyan, reflecting what seemed to be his genuine belief in Marxist ideology, responded in surprise: "If businessmen do not exercise such power, then who does?"

Every executive present argued, in one way or another and with utmost sincerity, that the most important single source of power in the United States at that time was organized labor. Their responses were well buttressed with examples of labor's influence in elections, in obtaining legislation, and in wielding influence over wages and benefits for workers that was probably excessive. The unity displayed, without benefit of briefing or collusion, must have made an impression on the guest of honor, who seemed distressed. He observed that U.S. businessmen obviously no longer know what a capitalist is!

A recitation and analysis of the views about union power held by a committee of executives, economists, and other advisers might be as instructive for thoughtful Americans as it was for the longest-serving late member of the Politburo. Such a group was recruited to prepare a policy statement on the issue of union power.

A STUDY BY THE EXPERTS AND THE REACTION TO IT

U.S. executives' state of consciousness about labor problems was sharpened by an effort, begun two years earlier, "to face up to the labor problem" – a cause dear to James D. Zellerbach who had retired from the chairmanship of the CED to become ambassador to Italy. A special fund had been raised to finance a no-strings-attached study by a group of independent labor relations experts chaired by Clark Kerr, then president of the University of California.[2] The independent study group contained the country's leading labor economists and experts. Its rapporteur was George P. Schultz, then a professor at the University of Chicago who later, despite his role in the study, became, successively, President Richard Nixon's director of the Office of Management and Budget, secretary of labor, secretary of the treasury, and later an adviser to President Ronald Reagan and president of the Bechtel Group Inc.

The study was intended to provide the background for a statement to be made by a group of executives who had been briefed by the authors of the study in a half-day presentation before it was published. While general agreement could not be expected on a wide-ranging review of public policies on labor organizations and collective bargaining, the thoughtful comments of the executives about the experts' study provided no clue to the reaction that followed its publication. Executives who were trustees of the organization began to receive letters from business people all over the country attacking the legitimacy of the publication (and sometimes the parentage of its authors), alleging a conspiracy by the authors and the staff to force compulsory unionism on the country. Many business people who objected to the study threatened to boycott companies whose executives were responsible for it unless the study were repudiated and withdrawn from circulation. Most letters urged the addressee to discontinue support of the culprit organization. It soon became clear that a single-purpose lobbying organization, which in succeeding years was to have many counterparts, had mounted and orchestrated the attack with some aid and encouragement from the National Association of Manufacturers, then under a management that was soon to disappear in a reorganization.

The focus of the attack was a suggestion in the study that a provision in federal law permitting negotiation of union shop agreements should prevail over another provision that permitted states to enact right-to-work laws restricting the negotiation of union shop agreements. The study by the experts further suggested that the federal law be amended to ensure that a "conscientious objector" who refused to join a union retain the right to hold his job if he were willing to pay a fee equivalent to union dues and fees for the services rendered by the union representing him and his fellow employees — an arrangement known as the "agency shop." The experts' study also suggested that federal law be amended to ensure "right of entry" into a labor organization by all qualified persons "regardless of race, creed, color, national origin, political beliefs or family ties,"[3] a matter then not covered in federal law but now required by equal employment opportunity legislation.

The disturbance created by the attack brought to fruition David Zellerbach's long campaign to get his colleagues to undertake in their own names a serious study of union-employer relations and collective bargaining. While the result of their effort was not noteworthy,[4] it did lift the taboo on the subject, which came to be discussed frequently by the group in subsequent years. It is from these discussions that much of this chapter on executive and professional ideology is drawn. The writer confesses to telescoping the time dimension in this chapter and to placing ideas in juxtaposition even though they were expressed several years apart. In justification, it can be argued that many of the same persons participated in both early and later discussions and that often they said the same things in meetings held several years apart. Their attitudes remained the same and were applied in essentially the same legal framework, there having been no fundamental change in labor legislation during the period. The state of the economy fluctuated from time to time, and labor relations would come under discussion whenever the inflation rate accelerated.

THE BASIC APPROACH TO LABOR PROBLEMS

Concern about the right-to-work issue may have triggered a facing up to the labor problem, but that issue was not important in the discussions of executives. The issue that they worried about most was, first and foremost, how anything they might say could be believed and understood by any but fellow business people. And how could anything they might say make any difference?

While much time and talk was devoted to this concern, discussion began and ended with one question: What convincing argument can we use that is in the public interest — that is good for the economy of the country? Whether entirely sincere, there was no doubt that any proposition had to meet that standard, if only on the pragmatic ground that nothing else had a chance to be believed by the public. A labor economist adviser who was an ardent champion of unions argued that the public interest test would be satisfied by an affirmation that the U.S. economy had provided the highest standard of living for the largest number of people in the history of the world, a boast that unfortunately is no longer fully supportable. It should be the intent of any labor policy, he argued, to continue that system. In milder terms, his position was reaffirmed at the time by most business people.

Defining the *public interest* was an easy task for economists and executives so long as it was confined to a generality. The standard of living is raised, almost everyone argued, by improving productivity, which is the basis for real economic growth. And improvement of productivity is the business of management, government, and labor alike, with emphasis on the qualification that just working harder is not what is called for. Improving productivity entails working more intelligently, incorporating training and skilled use of more machinery — both of which call for capital.

From this lofty consensus the argument becomes more convoluted and dissonant. It was the competitive system, most participants argued, that produced the happy outcome of higher productivity, higher incomes, and — an opinion that was much divided — more equitable distribution of income. It was on the combination of these propositions that the major ideological splits occurred.

FUNCTIONS OF THE UNIONS

To learn how unions fit into a competitive economy or, conversely, distort it, it is necessary to know what functions (according to people inside and outside the labor movement) unions seek to perform and how well they perform them. In an attempt to do justice to this question, I called on one of the AFL-CIO's (American Federation of Labor and Congress of Industrial Organizations) leading economists, told him what we were trying to find out, and asked if his organization had a statement or study about union functions — something that might be given to members, or groups being organized, or used in legislative hearings. He responded that there was no such statement available but that it was an interesting idea and that perhaps they should do something along those lines. He reminded me, however, that his job was to make the case that best represents the interests of organized labor, not necessarily to make an economically sound analysis.

Having received little help from union sources, we reviewed the literature, listened to the experts, and plumbed our own knowledge and prejudices on the question of union functions, with some interesting results.

A theoretical economist, to whom I shall refer frequently, argued that labor organization was a residue from the government's recovery program under the National Recovery Administration (NRA) of the 1930s during which both industry and labor were encouraged to unite for common action. He was promptly corrected by a top-ranking labor economist who claimed that in the United States from the time industry began, there had been continuous warfare between employers and labor over whether collective bargaining should be allowed. For 100 years it had been left to economic power to resolve the issue. Workers refused to accept the idea that a competitive economic system called for each worker to haggle individually with his employer over wages and working conditions. Instead, workers often chose to organize and be represented in the competition by a union. The important question was whether that union was concomitant with the problems to be solved. In saying this, he provided a key to the fundamental question on which we came to concentrate in later discussions.

Executives and professionals both alluded many times to the insecurity not of the union but of the individual worker and what this meant for union policy. There was no important disagreement with the notion that (as an executive of a unionized company said) the people of this country are not going to have their livelihood depend on the charity and paternalism of a small group of managers. Another executive noted soberly that he had observed that a person had little security under management unless someone could represent him in some kind of appeal, with benefit of independent counseling such as that supplied by a union.

The most poignant of many conversations I have had with labor leaders about the function of unions had to do with the problem of adjustment assistance to workers who lost jobs because of import competition. "Why," asked the union leader, "do workers always have to do most of the adjusting?" His union colleague added the more difficult question: "When one of my members who has lost his job because of imports comes to me and I explain what is meant by adjusting and he asks, 'Well, what do I tell my wife when I go home tonight?' — what do I say to him?"

The head of one of the country's largest companies put the question into broader context.

> The way we get things done in this country is by organizing our efforts. We do this in management, in government, and in labor relations. A large corporation requires an organization on the labor side with which it can coordinate its effort. But there is competition among groups and the question is, Are labor organizations in some of our industries insulated from competition and does that situation produce the best results?

One of his large competitors extended his philosophy, saying:

> I doubt that we would gain much if we decertified unions in all of our plants overnight — or even in one of them. The important thing is being able to deal with our employees as a group; our biggest problem is establishing good relations with representatives in each plant. Sometimes there is a great advantage in having a union if you can negotiate with it on the basis of an economic understanding of industry's problems. To whom otherwise are you going to talk? If I understand industry today, I don't think it is necessarily antiunion. What we would like is better union understanding of the economic facts of life and of our management problems.

(He did not, nor did his compatriots, say anything about how far companies should attempt to share management policy making with union representatives. It was 15 years later that the president of the United Auto Workers requested and obtained membership on the Chrysler board of directors. Companies in

Germany have long had such a practice, and now labor representatives constitute half the membership of large company supervisory boards in Germany.)

A senior labor economist put the issue into a still larger frame by adding that unions might assume a larger role in management problems and exercise more restraint in the interest of the people they represent. There is emerging, he said prophetically, a view that unions in their bargaining must take into account national necessities – control of inflation, for example. There is quite a difference between the functions unions perform if they are merely working with management to get a viable company or working with management and government to get a viable economy. (Union leadership and management were later to serve together on a presidential pay advisory board, as they had during World War II.)

Another executive made a telling argument about why in the inflationary 1970s it was so difficult for organized labor to fulfill the larger function just described. With little more than a quarter of the labor force organized, he said, the only way that unions can justify their position and obtain a sense of security is to get more per organized worker than they could otherwise get. Union leaders reaffirm their position and their worth by getting more than they should, so that they and their people can always point this out when they are trying to get new workers organized. He concluded with what he thought would be considered a crazy idea: Maybe if all working people were members of some kind of union, they could intelligently work with us to do a better job for all, rather than reaffirming their security in a situation where only one out of four working people is actually in their ranks. He concluded, So long as they are fundamentally insecure, they are not going to be responsible.

The importance of union security was demonstrated to some of us serving on an international economic policy commission when the head of a union representing workers in a high-technology industry that was very competitive in the export market voted with another union leader, whose members were losing jobs to imports, in favor of the protectionist Burke-Hartke bill. When the leader of the export-oriented union was asked why he favored something that was probably contrary to the interests of his union's own members, he replied, "*Union solidarity!*"

In a discursive way, the foregoing discussion of the functions of unions indicates that the views expressed by a group of executives may be both humanistic and not necessarily antiunion. The views in the next section on the economic effects of unions are more stringent and represent the economists' judgment to a much greater degree than that of executives who are not specialists in macroeconomics.

ECONOMIC EFFECTS OF UNION POWER

The classic case against union power is that it enables some groups of workers to gain at the expense of others or of society as a whole – to rob Peter to pay Paul. The theoretical economists argued that the ability of powerful unions to push up wages excessively must be at the expense of the unorganized because higher wages in organized industries result in less employment there, and workers who might otherwise be employed in those industries must seek jobs and compete with the unorganized in other occupations. This would tend to hold down the wages of the unorganized and leads to the conclusion that strongly organized workers obtain their higher wages at the expense of others — particularly of other workers — because wages constitute more than three-fourths of the national income.[5]

This set of theoretical propositions on the surface seems persuasive, but the discussions illustrated some differences of opinion (and of knowledge) not always apparent to the participants.

The economy, after all, has to operate within a constitutional framework of individual freedom, including the right of association — a right that is not negotiable. The very existence of a union as a bargaining unit controls the supply of labor to an employer. The discussion participants agreed that in this country it is not possible to return to the practice of each individual worker's bargaining for wages. We must distinguish between competition among individual workers and competition among unions. What this line of argument means is that executives, by and large, do not consider outlawing unions to be a realistic alternative, regardless of alleged distortions of income distribution because of union activity.

Implications of the argument that strongly unionized workers gain at the expense of others also failed to stand up in practice because of the very important proviso that wage gains by such unions may be offset by productivity increases. If higher wages are not offset sooner or later by increased productivity, then why do higher wages in a particular industry often lead to reductions in the company's work force? Such reductions are the way companies reorganize to make productivity of the remaining workers rise to equal their higher pay. In case after case, executives complained that they were driven into automation, forced to close down high-cost plants, retrain workers, and do many other things to offset the increased wage costs forced upon them. These adjustments are, of course, part of the process by which increased productivity is brought about, and the process is often accompanied by layoffs in the short run. The pressure of collectively bargained wage increases may well be an element in how productivity gains are accelerated in the private sector and also part of the process by which the labor force is redeployed into the sectors of the economy where jobs are increasing. This process occurs in the model of a growing economy in which total employment is increasing.

There is another pervasive form of productivity improvement that unions have demonstratively accelerated. It is to improve the hours and conditions of work. One executive of a high-employment retail industry argued that labor should be given credit for forcing business into many greater efficiencies and especially into better handling and development of personnel. An economist executive noted that until union pressures were applied, the hours of work were "sun up to sun down" – a work day that proved over time to have been inefficient in terms of labor output per hour or per day. As early as World War I, shorter work days were mandated by governments in several countries to increase worker productivity. Similarly, early health and accident legislation proved to have positive productivity effects, much of which was reflected in reduced absenteeism, lower accident insurance premiums, and lower social costs of health care. These gains were not confined to unionized companies.

UNION POWER AND ECONOMIC STABILITY

Ever since the Great Depression of the 1930s, when a vast majority of economists had little or nothing to contribute to the then unfamiliar concept of national stabilization policy, there has been serious concern about government and private policies that would encourage high-level stability of the economy. As earlier chapters have noted, in the circle not only of economists but also of business people, there was in the decades after World War II growing disquietude about the appropriate role of organized labor in achieving the hybrid set of goals calling for steady growth, full employment, price stability, and balance-of payments-equilibrium.

In recent years, the freeing of the dollar to depreciate in terms of foreign currencies has reduced the theoretical importance of balance-of-payments problems – after actual payments deficits became more important – because exchange rate depreciation was expected to compensate for excessive wage costs. Under a flexible exchange rate system, capital flows, energy price increases, and shocks other than wage increases would have to provide an explanation for U.S. balance-of-payments deficits. And, as I have shown earlier, the lagging rate of investment, a declining rate of savings, and the mandatory diversion of investment funds into such uses as control of pollution, mitigation of hazards in the workplace, and adaptation to high energy costs go a long way toward explaining the slowdown in domestic economic growth.

But the contradictory situation that is characterized by intractable inflation accompanied by a relatively high rate of unemployment focuses attention on the macroeconomic effects of the power of labor organizations over wages. Any serious study of union powers and functions would have to consider this question, but in doing so it would have to lean heavily upon the work of economists because business people in this country have had little experience with the new state of affairs.

Our theoretical economist mentors were prepared to make a case that union power contributed to inflation, unemployment, and even lesser maladies of the body economic even when three-quarters of the labor force is not unionized. The so-called Phillips curve related decreased unemployment to rising inflation; the process of reducing unemployment seemed to generate a wage-price spiral. To many economists and others, the wage pressures of unions became the villains in these developments. In recent times the staggered expiration of labor contracts tended to make each contract renewal match the highest prior settlement obtained by other unions, with each settlement being passed on through higher costs into higher prices.

Some of our economist mentors argued that emergence of this situation demonstrated that businesses and labor organizations are able to raise prices and wage rates without being subject to the market penalties imposed by lower sales and lower employment. Under these conditions a solution could be sought through rigorous, even radical, measures to strengthen competition, although what this would require is never spelled out. Business has long been subject to antitrust laws, but labor organizations have not. Since labor has been free to form unions that can cover not only a single industry but several industries, and since wages make up the bulk of business costs, it seems clear, at least to some economists, that priority should be given to the possibility of restricting organized labor's power to force wages up.

What does the preceding analysis mean? First, it means that the argument that unions in periods of relatively stable prices secure gains at the expense of others may have some truth in it but is not particularly relevant under conditions of inflation. Second, it means that in a period of inflation the power of strong unions to obtain wage increases as their contracts expire can either accelerate or delay cost-push inflation. So long as wages covered by contracts do not automatically escalate, as with cost-of-living adjustments (COLAs) and large automatic increases in excess of COLA, they can slow down wage cost escalation because the agreement stabilized wages for the term of the contract. But as new contracts are made, and to the extent that they contain COLA and increases in wages based upon an anticipated inflation rate, they can accelerate the inflation process. This possibility will be considered again in the final chapter.

Hard as it may be to separate the two, the role of unions in controlling inflation must somehow be considered separately from the question of union powers and functions under conditions of general price stability. It may well be that strong and responsible unions can become instruments for either reducing or increasing inflation; the power to accomplish the latter implies power to accomplish the former.

ABUSES OF UNION POWER

Any discussion by business executives of union power will always produce an outpouring of complaints about abuses of power. As this discussion was initiated by an independent study that questioned state right-to work-laws, the executive interest centered for a time on rights of the individual. Cases were cited of union hiring halls and their informal counterparts. In many skilled trades (lithographers, electricians, and pipefitters) in many areas, employers are restricted to hiring union members, and the number of new members permitted to enter the unions that follow such practices is limited. A major cause for complaint was that too often the union's supply of qualified members, especially in a tight labor market for the requisite skills, resulted in many underqualified or semiincompetents having to be hired. There was general agreement that the government was not the proper recourse in these situations; despite complaints, managements evidenced a strong preference to negotiate directly with the unions rather than to seek government laws or regulations.

More surprising, however, was the result of the discussion on right-to-work laws. It was authoritatively asserted by both professional and executive experts that the Taft-Hartley Act's provision outlawing the closed shop and the existing antidiscrimination legislation requiring unions to be open to all races, colors, creeds (and probably sexes) really covered the question, however much poor law enforcement might obscure the fact. The critical issue, according to a senior labor adviser, is giving a union exclusive rights to representation on all questions, including those having to do with equal opportunity. The group did not follow up this discussion except as it applied to compulsory payments of dues or fees to unions. The committee simply disposed of the right-to-work issue by endorsing the principle that no one should have to join a union or pay a fee to a union to get or keep a job. There was much support for an overriding federal, rather than individual state, standard on this matter because of the need to move workers and contractors around the country. Out-of-state union members called in to augment the local supply of skilled labor on large projects often objected to working with nonunion persons in right-to-work states.

The principal complaints voiced by executives in the matter of individual rights had to do with union practices that they considered a violation of the rights of union members. Leading examples were the union practices limiting or controlling the number of apprentices and their training, supplying incompetent workers, insisting that an excessive number of workers be hired (featherbedding), and using strong-arm or similar tactics to prevent the membership from voting on employers' offers. No sweeping reforms were suggested, and further government intervention was to be eschewed, but some interesting observations were made about union democracy.

The executives complained about such failures of democratic procedure as submitting to a vote of the membership some employer's offer that the union leadership had rejected; nevertheless, they backed away from endorsing such democratic procedures as a secret ballot by members on contracts that were acceptable to union leadership.

The corporate executives were keenly aware that anything said about democracy in unions could also be said about democracy in corporations. Most large companies, said one, are run by a few people — sometimes only one person. As one politically experienced executive put it in a later discussion, the only product of making unions more democratic would be a counterrevolution about making business management more democratic. It seems, said he, that if we support that idea, we are treading unnecessarily on an awful lot of eggs. A colleague with similar background observed that there were many employers who would like to see stronger and more responsible union leadership and less democracy. A spokesman for the group summarized its views on this issue, saying, We finally decided that it really isn't any of our business how the unions are run; we are not qualified to set up a pattern on how to run unions. So much for union democracy.

UNION POLITICAL ACTIVITY

The attitude and reasoning about union political activity was quite another matter than that about internal union democracy. Everyone was already aware, or soon found out, that union funds could be funneled through political action committees and that union staff and members could work actively in political campaigns and lobbying. While direct union and corporate contributions to federal election campaigns had long been prohibited, by the 1970s it was permissible in 31 states for union funds collected in those states to be channeled through state labor organizations into federal political campaigns as well as into campaigns in their own states. The final policy statement, issued in 1964 by the labor study committee of executives, recommended prohibiting such uses of union resources. But in a 1968 statement on election reform, a group containing many of the same executives came up with a different recommendation: that corporations and unions be treated alike with respect to political contributions and activities, both of which should remain illegal in federal elections. Equality of treatment, however, also meant that if unions were permitted to encourage political action committees voluntarily supported by the contributions of members and employees of the organization, corporations should be permitted to do the same.

The reform of election and campaign financing laws and regulations in 1974 accorded business the same channel for campaign contributions that, a few years earlier, it had inveighed against when the practice was exercised by labor organizations. Now, members of unions, stockholders, executives and administrative employees of corporations, and business and professional groups as well as labor organizations may be solicited and may contribute to political action committees (PACs), which may use the funds to support the campaigns of candidates. Each PAC is allowed to put up a maximum of $5,000 for a candidate in each primary, runoff, and general election campaign. The old "fat-cat" campaign contribution (formerly in wide use) was cut down to no more than $1,000 per candidate per election. By August, 1978 labor PACs numbered only 266, according to the Federal Election Commission, but corporations and business-related associations had grown to nearly 1,500. Under the new rules, business PACs reportedly spent $21 million in the 1978 election, whereas labor PACs spent only half that amount. By June 30, 1980, for the 1980 campaign business PACs had raised $23 million and labor PACs only $17.5 million.[6]

With expensive television and other media campaigns becoming more decisive in elections, we may expect that the strong protests of business in the 1960s about labor financing of election campaigns will not soon be repeated. The faiure of organized labor's campaign for reform of federal labor legislation in 1978, in a Democratic Congress, was undoubtedly influenced by the PAC-dollar-contributions derby. Business related PACs outnumber labor related ones and can easily expand their numbers to ensure a volume of support for candidates exceeding that of labor related PACs.[7]

LABOR STRIFE AND VIOLENCE

Commenting on the use of violence in strikes, the chief executive of a major company remarked that if it is wrong, we should not condone it.

Throughout the discussions on labor relations, all participants condemned violence as a tool in labor disputes. All agreed that laws were not enough. Enforcement of laws was lacking. Everybody, said one, should have the right to cross a picket line if he wants to, but the law enforcement officers won't help you do it.

The principle is simple: If it is wrong, we should not condone it. No one made the connection between that principle and the policies pursued by business itself. Corporate behavior displays an astonishing ambivalence about law enforcement. So as not to complicate the issue, we will put to one side the illegal campaign contributions and corporate bribery ("questionable payments") to obtain sales that have been recently in the news.

A specialist in government pointed out that in their internal affairs many, if not most, companies prefer to be self-policing — especially on illegal matters that they prefer not to have prosecuted. Embezzlement by a trusted officer or employee, for example, is seldom prosecuted if, after discovery, there is restitution and resignation by the culprit. But even more flagrant disrespect for law is widespread and condoned. On many of the automobile industry's assembly lines, workers can use drugs with impunity so long as they do not disrupt operations. Illegal gambling and loan sharking are common in many plants. In cases of larceny or burglary of expensive jewelry, the insurers often condone fencing, buying back the stolen property at a fraction of its value, sometimes in cooperation with the police. Overinsurance of buildings against fire and casualty losses is alleged to have encouraged arson.

Business has a role to play in cooperation with government in fostering respect for an impartial application of laws. The counterpart of violence on the picket line is violation of the law on the production line and in the office.

HOW TO BELL THE UNION CAT

While the preceding pages illustrate the wide range of topics discussed, the crux of the discussion kept coming back to the question of union power. There was agreement on the principle that union powers ought to be commensurate with their functions. Union representation of members in settling grievances, training programs, or political action could be accommodated by a variety of union sizes and structures. The central issue was the kind of union structure and size needed for bargaining over economic issues.

The theoretical economist argued that it was probably illegal for a group of steel companies to get together and agree to buy all their coal from one coal company but perfectly all right for the same group of companies to get together to buy labor services through one union. In simple terms, this was the argument for applying the antitrust laws to unions.

Some executives of large industrial companies translated this proposal to mean that a union should be restrained from bargaining over wage and related issues with more than one company. The proposal was thoughtfully attacked by other executives on several grounds. Suppose, one asked, the various one-company unions in an industry came up with the same demands or insisted on the same settlement as that obtained by another union in another company — could this be collusion in violation of the antitrust law?

Executives and others familiar with bargaining in the construction industry found unacceptable the proposal to confine a union to representation of the workers of only a single company. In the construction industry there are 19 or more national unions, each with several hundred locals bargaining with thousands of employers. In this industry employers and students of the problem have worked for years to extend the size of the bargaining unit on both sides as a means of eliminating wildly inflationary local settlements and sporadic, irresponsible strikes by a single union, which could, and often did, close down major operations and escalate costs.

The airlines industry was cited by the senior labor adviser as an example of single-company bargaining with fragmented unions. The system has in bad times resulted in instability and whipsawing of unions by companies and in good times of companies by unions.

An executive of a multiplant company observed that he could see nothing in the proposal that would prevent sympathy strikes by unions representing other companies in an industry if one union struck one company. The head of one of the nation's largest companies, which had been cited often for alleged violations of antitrust laws, rejected the proposal for one-company unions on the ground that if the antitrust laws were to apply to unions and be enforced as they are against businesses, it would be a fate that he would not wish even an enemy to endure.

In the end, this and similar proposals to limit the scope of union jurisdiction over representation were rejected because they curtailed the freedom of the employer to work out his own bargaining relations with unions and the freedom of individuals to join or not to join unions of their own choice.

The most original position of any executive was so striking that it is worth a paragraph.

We continue to temporize with antitrust laws developed in the nineteenth century, when we were a nation of small shopkeepers and farmers, and with concepts of trade unions developed in the 1930s and earlier, when unions were trying to establish themselves. As we face the rest of the world where competitors are unhampered by such laws and concepts, we ought to consider removing antitrust inhibitions on basic industries in which substantial economies and efficiencies are obtainable by concentration. If we did that, the concentrated industries would have to be regulated in much the way that AT&T is now regulated. Concurrently, on the labor side we would have arbitration of wages and other major economic benefits.

While no one, for the record, supported the whole of this statement, there was considerable support for the proposal that binding arbitration was a desirable means for settling wage disputes in situations involving large companies confronted by large unions. The group's report, however, was silent on this subject.

The discussions and the findings of the committee leaned strongly against increased government intervention to reshape the structures and processes of labor relations. They did not encompass any broad reforms that could be relied on to obviate government intervention to protect the public interest when labor disputes created a national emergency. Having failed in that, the group had no choice but to endorse the Taft-Hartley Act's provisions for dealing with disputes creating a national emergency — the 80-day "cooling off" period followed by submission of the employers' last offer to a vote of the union members if the dispute continued and, if that step failed, a last-resort presidential recommendation to Congress for action.

LABOR RELATIONS IN A BETTER WORLD

Scattered through many discussions, not only on labor policy but also on social responsibility, controlling inflation, and other issues, was a little dreaming by executives and advisers about a better world of labor relations.

Starting with the lowest rung of fantasy, several participants deplored the absence of high-level (for example, board of directors) concern about company employee relations except at times when labor negotiations were under way or strikes were threatened. Whether we are unionized or not, asked one company executive whose specialty was labor relations, don't we [top executives] have responsibility for our employees' understanding of the work relationships between employer and individual? Haven't we often failed to assume and discharge this responsibility?

A labor adviser reflected on the same question. Some of the best labor relations I know, he observed, are in nonunionized companies where workers have as good status in all respects as in some of the unioned companies. I am not talking about buying your way to good relations but about a modern personnel policy of discerning what people are after and providing them with it in different ways. This is something not outside your control to the extent that is usually assumed.

From other sources, the author knows of companies having good labor relations that nevertheless employ outside groups of applied psychologists to conduct in-depth interviews of cross sections of employees to ascertain incidents of employee satisfaction and dissatisfaction related to the workplace. From such sources in recent years have come experiments with flexitime — part-time work and equalization of the privileges of blue-collar workers with those of white-collar workers of time off for personal necessities such as doctor's appointments for family members.

WHO GETS PROMOTED TO EXECUTIVE LEVEL?

Another fundamental concern was raised by the head of a very large merchandizing organization. He cited the record of American Telephone and Telegraph (AT&T), which was very proud of its practice of bringing its top people up the ladder — all started as linemen or in similar jobs. He reported that in his own company nobody gets to the top unless he came in at the bottom. Now, he said, instead of having a policy that allows everyone to rise to a level that his talent, ability, and willingness allow, most companies are recruiting for management a trainee class brought in from the colleges and universities, bypassing the rank and file of organized workers who are becoming part of a fixed, flat, stratified society. Another executive agreed that in his experience very rarely did a fellow who starts on the bench in a factory every get a chance to enter the top management.

The executive of an automotive company reported that about half of the male salaried employees in his company were originally hourly workers and that many in management started that way. A basic materials company executive reported about the same percentages, as did a container manufacturer.

But there was no exception to the conclusion that the trend was toward filling more and more management positions from the trainee groups brought in from institutions of higher education. This, observed a top executive, is a trend that frightens me. And with good reason, because the trend has continued.

A recent comprehensive study of promotions to vice-president or president of 11,000 executives in 33 industries showed that the proportion with a high school education or less had fallen to 3 percent in 1976 from 6 percent in 1967 and 30 percent in 1950. In contrast, the proportion with a graduate degree (master's or higher) had risen from 20 percent in 1950 to 33 percent in 1967 and 41 percent in 1976.[8] The increased proportion of graduate degree holders was mainly the result of employing a larger number of persons having a master's in business administration.

UNION WAGE PRESSURES AND INFLATION

The inability of leaders in the private sector to generate an acceptable and workable program to stop the wage-price spiral represents one of the greatest and most conspicuous failures of this and other industrial democracies. It sets the agenda for the next two chapters.

Allan Sproul, former president of the Federal Reserve Bank of New York and a participant in the group that produced the labor policy statement, singled out in a published note its most important weakness. He commented that "it dismisses too cavalierly the interest and role of government in labor-management relations, quite apart from specific labor disputes, leaving a void with respect to the coordination of wage-price policies with fiscal and monetary policies designed to promote sustainable economic growth, which is one of the critical issues of our time."[9]

In the 1970s the inflationary spiral came to transcend such problems as union structure and functions or representation and rights of union members. But the ideological conflict between executives and advisers continued over how to curb accelerating inflation reinforced by the resumption of the wage-price spiral.

On this issue the theoretical economists managed to go underground or to group themselves more or less amicably into schools. Monetarists kept up a drumfire about money supply excesses but had little other than tight money and high interest rates to offer as tactics for a transition to wage-price stabilization. This at least provided the policy makers in government with a bogeyman: cooperate with guidelines or we will have a real depression. Unfortunately, as has been noted earlier, the bogeyman materialized in the 1973/75 and 1980/81 recessions.

The advocates of a return to laissez-faire rather lamely trotted out the case for a fundamental restructuring of the economy to restore competition in all markets — the intellectual foundation for the proposal to apply antitrust laws to labor organizations.

Their nearest intellectual relatives contented themselves with wide-ranging proposals for structural changes designed to remove impediments to competition (including much government regulation) wherever they are found to be important contributors to inflationary pressures.

Examples include removing restrictions on training people in skills that are in short supply, delaying increases in the minimum wage, repealing the Bacon-Davis Act, opening more public lands to timber cutting and oil exploration, and making people on strike ineligible for unemployment benefits or welfare in states where this is permitted (for example, New York and Rhode Island).[10] These, while mostly sensible long-range measures, promised little for the immediate future.

In its latest policy statements on inflation, the committee concentrated on monetary and fiscal policies supplemented by a broad program of structural changes and other measures to improve productivity. They rejected both incomes policies and wage and price controls. In calling for structural changes to increase competition, they incurred the disfavor of a number of executives of large companies, including important members of the Business Roundtable, a companion organization of executives devoted to the promotion of what its members considered to be sound public policies. One important member of that group took an uncompromisingly negative view of the arguments supporting the structural change approach as it applied to big business. In a conversation with me, he said (I think mostly in jest) that if one objectionable passage in a policy statement were not changed, he might have to advise his colleagues to reduce or terminate their support of the organization. (In fact, he did nothing of the kind.) The passage in dispute is reproduced below, with italics added by the author.

> Price reductions in recessions have also been moderated by the operation of restrictive trade laws, by the sensitivity of Western countries to demands for quota protection in certain industries where both management and labor are politically active, and *by limited price competition in those markets where the presence of few firms cannot be explained by economies of scale in production and distribution.*[11]

TAX MEASURES TO CONTROL THE WAGE-PRICE SPIRAL

The boldest proposals for short-run policies to curb wage-price inflation came from sources that had no particular ideological tag except possibly policy-making experience in government. Most of these proposals are premised upon an explicit standard for moderating the rate of increase in wages and prices without imposing direct controls. The most notable is probably that of Henry C. Wallich, presently a member of the board of governors of the Federal Reserve System. Wallich proposed a special tax on corporations granting excessive wage increases. Such a tax is designed to stiffen corporate resistance to excessive union wage demands, even to the point of taking a long and expensive strike to do it (the General Electric model of 1969/70). It could include a tax on companies that exceeded the wage standard, and the tax base could be profits or payrolls — a profits tax being preferred because it politically balances the restriction on wage increases. The wage guideline could be the national productivity gain plus an inflation rate of the recent past but lower than the current rate. Implicitly Wallich assumes that the business and labor power structures have come to collaborate on excessive wage increases that can be passed on in higher prices; the tax is designed to make such behavior costly to business and less rewarding for labor. Wallich has rejected a tax on the excessive part of a wage increase itself because the political pressure of labor's opposition could defeat the plan.

The executives' reaction to this proposal was, as might be expected, generally negative because companies would be hit twice in consequence of what they regarded as excessive labor power — first by unions and then by the tax penalty. And to take a strike was, they argued, to lose (with help from imports) a considerable part of a market share built up by years of effort and investment as well as the goodwill of the company's workers and many of its customers.

But out of such considerations was born the Carter plan of November 1978, which substituted for the stick of a tax increase on profits the carrot of real wage insurance for labor cooperation with a wage guideline. Some type of tax-based incomes policy (TIP) that rewards wage restraint might succeed if the power structures of business, labor, and government could find ways to work together to carry it out, but as of 1981 few would contend that the three parts of the power structure could achieve the degree of cooperation that is necessary. I will have much to say later about power structures and cooperation.

OTHER TRADE-OFFS TO STOP THE SPIRAL

In a discussion on the inflation of the 1970s, an executive with much political and government experience raised the critical issue about national economic policies that generated a virulent attack of wage-price spiralitis. Maybe, he mused, we ought to look at labor's attitudes toward keeping ahead of inflation and see if there is something that labor wants that will make it politically acceptable to labor to change its position.

It was duly noted that labor's first concern is high employment, to which the country has been long committed, so that uniting on that goal offers little trade-off. Some trade-off might be available in providing better job security, but that, too, is largely achieved by the commitment to national high employment and support for the unemployed at improving levels — for example, by company-financed supplementary unemployment benefits (SUBs).

The big trade-off — perhaps too big and too far in the future — might be the statesman executive's suggestion described earlier that all employees belong to some kind of independent organization of their choice. In the end that may be the winning combination.

A more moderate but also more easily achieved trade-off might be national health insurance. There is probably no greater insecurity for workers, especially the laid off or unemployed, than expiration of employer-paid or partially paid health insurance, or lack of any coverage at all. A national health insurance program is high on organized labor's legislative agenda. It is the largest unmet need for attaining a better quality of life. With the right kind of structure such a system need not add an insupportable burden to the federal budget. Medicare for the elderly and Medicaid for the poor — the most expensive parts of a national system — are already in place and in the federal budget.

There is, however, a dreamlike quality to all proposals for trade-offs with labor to promote the public interest. The essential elements in a trade-off process do not exist. Who, and with what legitimacy, is to represent labor, organized and unorganized? Who will represent management of all the diverse private businesses of the country? And who will commit the government's executive and legislative branches that would have to deliver on the government's promises? There is neither organization, procedure, nor precedent for carrying out any nationwide bargain among the parts of the power structure. If workable national policies depend upon such bargaining, then a framework for conducting it is yet to be created.

The situation just described is virtually unique to the United States. Japan and the principal industrial democracies of Europe have parliamentary systems capable of committing their governments, subject, of course, to their being turned out of power by the electorate. Their principal employer and employee groups are represented by monolithic organizations capable of negotiating on behalf of their member groups. Some countries – for example, Germany and Sweden – have used some form of national wage bargain tempered by their leaders' recognition that any bargain they make must be acceptable to a majority of the electorate.

NOTES

1. The material summarized here is derived from a personal memorandum of the author.

2. Committee for Economic Development, *The Public Interest in National Labor Policy* (New York: CED, 1961).

3. Ibid. For a fuller discussion, see pp. 150-52.

4. Committee for Economic Development, *Union Powers and Union Functions: Toward a Better Balance* (New York: CED, 1964).

5. This conclusion is derived from the favorite model of economists: a competitive economy into which a strong union is introduced. The monopolistic power of the union is allowed to increase wages above the competitive level, and unionized employers are permitted to reduce the labor component in their combination of the factors of production in response to higher wages. Workers unemployed as a result are permitted to undercut unorganized workers, who in consequence also must accept sufficiently lower wages to "clear the market" of the unemployed. Virtually all other changes, except changes in prices of products induced by wage changes, are excluded from the analysis.

6. Federal Election Commission, reported in the *New York Times*, September 25, 1980, pp. 8-10.

7. Edwin M. Epstein, "The Emergence of Political Action Committees," in *Political Finance*, ed. Herbert A. Alexander, Sage Electoral Studies Yearbook, vol. 5 (Beverly Hills: Sage Publications, 1979), pp. 183-191.

8. These comparative statistics are derived from Alfred W. Swinyard and Floyd A. Bond, "Who Gets Promoted?" *Harvard Business Review* (September-October 1980) pp. 6-18.

9. Committee for Economic Development, *Union Powers and Union Functions.*

10. The Supreme Court of the United States on March 21, 1979, upheld state laws making workers on strike eligible for unemployment benefits. See *New York Telephone Co.* v. *New York State Department of Labor* (77-961).

11. Committee for Economic Development, *Fighting Inflation and Promoting Growth* (New York: CED, 1976).

7

CORPORATE SIZE AND
COST–PRICE BEHAVIOR

In discussions that occurred during and after the 1973-75 recession, the chief executive of a large firm producing industrial products took heated exception to the frequent contentions of economists that in a recession the prices of most products with reduced demand should be expected to be cut. In fact, this was not happening.

We are, the executive said, one of the largest and the lowest-cost of six or seven producers of X, a chemical that enters into upholstery coverings. Product X amounts to less than 10 percent of the value of the products into which it enters. It doesn't make any sense for the company to reduce the price of X, which is a negligible part of the price of the final products containing it. He continued, My company is an almost sole source of domestic supply for another chemical product, Y, which is an essential component of equipment for automobiles and trucks but which, again, amounts to a very low percentage of their total cost. Once more he argued that to cut his company's price could bring about no benefits. To cut prices of X or Y would only reduce earnings; lower earnings would reduce funds for the kind of investment that would allow the company to produce at even lower costs and thereby to cut prices in the future.

As almost the sole producer of one product and one of few producers of the other, he argued further that his competitors would match his price cuts anyway, that they knew this, and that no one would gain anything. Speaking for many of his colleagues, he concluded with the fervent wish that economists would get off his back about cutting such prices as a response to falling demand.

In these cases, it should be noted that need for economies of scale limited the number of producers and plants. In the case of product Y, lowest cost would be obtained with a single plant's meeting the total demand. In both cases, the executive's company had the discretion to cut prices or even to raise them, despite falling demand.

While products X and Y are exceptional cases because each depends on derived demand for the product into which it enters, each is not exceptional in being produced by a small number of firms, none of which could expect to increase sales by means of a price cut that would simply be matched by others.

Another executive alluded to price rebates on automobiles, noting that Chrysler and American Motors were the first to announce them and General Motors the last — with good reason, he said. What would be the advantage, he asked, if Chrysler went broke? One of his colleagues added, If your company was in the top quarter of an industry in size and profits, it could by cutting prices subject itself to a serious antitrust charge. It is a somewhat surprising anomaly that antitrust laws designed to enhance price competition can have the effect of suppressing it.

In a different discussion another executive noted that a low-cost producer, who is probably a predominant producer, could by cutting prices put other firms out of business. Don't think I haven't thought of it, he said, because I could put a lot of people out of business. I don't think it would be good policy to do that. And, added a colleague, if you did cut your prices, the Department of Justice would take you to task anyway.

Still another participant (less subtle than most) expressed his surprise that economists looked on price cutting in recession as a means of getting rid of excess high-cost capacity. We can't, he said. It stays right with us, sometimes run by others. Besides, with a reduction in volume and all that excess capacity on hand, we ought to raise prices to cover the cost of idle investment so that it remains available when the recession is over; otherwise, somewhere down the road we will find ourselves with old plants and high costs because we have not earned enough depreciation to keep modern, and the competition will eat us up.

Much later, as though picking up a loose thread of the preceding argument, the producer of a variety of mobile machinery for both national and international markets took on the issue of cutting prices to sustain volume in his high fixed-cost industry. Economists don't appreciate that much of variable costs, like wages, have become fixed in the sense that layoffs and reduced production do not reduce them. In his and other industries under the same type of labor contracts, layoffs result in continuation of wages and fringes (which may amount to as much as 75 to 80 percent of wages) for a considerable time — upward of a year for wages and longer for fringes. He admitted that many U.S. industries were facing a disguised form of the Japanese company's lifetime commitment to employees to keep them on the job.

Another thoughtful executive concluded, These are some of the reasons why throwing the economy into increased unemployment to correct an inflation won't work. Prices don't decline in a recession. Another added, And if what we have heard about price elasticity is right, coming out a recession will be considered a very good time to raise prices because at that time it will not affect your volume. A primary metals producer agreed, if in an earlier period your prices were held down by controls or governmental arm-twisting (as was the case in the period under discussion) you would have to raise prices in a recovery when you could make them stick, especially if wage adjustments had gone on as the cost of living went up.

WHY ACTUAL DIFFERS FROM EXPECTED PRICE BEHAVIOR

A perceptive economist summed up the discussion and the attitudes that had surfaced in some cogent remarks that he later had opportunity to test in a high government position.

There have been changes in the U.S. economic system that have made debatable the analogy of a competitive economy where demand and supply are supposed to operate to dampen price movements. One reason is that relative price changes do not result, as they are supposed to, in prices going up on goods whose demand has gone up or in prices declining on goods for which demand has gone down. Instead, prices of most producers tend to stay constant or even rise a little bit along with the upward trend of other prices following an increase in demand. So almost by definition *all increases in relative prices are inflationary*, and relative price increases almost always drive up the price level because they are not offset by price reductions on other goods. [The Organization of Petroleum Exporting Countries (OPEC) oil price increases have had this effect.]

The key change that has occurred in our economic system that is responsible for such behavior is the organization of powerful interest groups within the economic system. Many want to focus the argument on labor unions, but interest groups extend far beyond labor unions to professional organizations among doctors and lawyers, the whole medical industry as it is now organized, unionized public-sector workers, and closely organized industries.

A second major factor is the series of technological changes that have made a lot of things inevitable and irreversible. The technological changes requiring automation, large-scale plants and large work forces probably dictate acceptance of labor unions which provide some coherent way of dealing with the work force and giving it a feeling that it has got some control over its environment. [Without his realizing it, his view corresponds to that of the executives summarized in the preceding chapter.]

A third major factor has been an intermingling of the political and economic arenas. Most Americans don't really believe that there is any longer a competitive U.S. economy in which individual workers can attempt in the marketplace to earn the rewards that they think are due them. When people don't achieve the rewards they consider rightfully theirs, they simply organize or turn to the political arena and try to win the fight there.

The economist then summed up his case [in what is now called post-Keynesian terms.[1]] The competitive market economy is supposed to determine relative prices, and the overall price level is supposed to be determined by aggregate money demand relative to total supply. But with the present structure of the economy, when demand falls, prices do not; the amount of output falls and unemployment increases. Considering the experience of the last two recessions, 1973-75 and 1980/81, it must be concluded that reliance on restrictive monetary and fiscal politics to hold down price inflation is unacceptable. Some policy makers and business executives may regard the cost as worthwhile, but the overwhelming majority of the population does not. If some of these tactics to correct stagflation are continued, there will be more intervention of the political system into the economic arena — and more and more intervention, because the market does not work the way economists assume that it would.

Were it not for the findings of broad-based studies of price and cost behavior in a series of recent recessions, the views of large-company executives about their firms' price behavior might be considered isolated special cases — artifacts. As has been shown earlier, however, margins over direct costs in the more concentrated industries behaved very much as though the views of executives cited above were in fact the common basis for pricing decisions. In recessions accompanied by inflation, prices of the largest firms were either maintained when direct costs went down or even raised by more than when direct costs went up. This behavior pattern is also becoming increasingly prevalent in the less concentrated industries, which in previous times showed narrowing margins in recessions.

The significance of the views and behavior just discussed depends on how important large firms are in the economy. If the bulk of the economy is composed of large firms whose pricing decisions in stagflation are made as executives have described and as the price-cost-margin studies bear out, then effective stabilization policies must be quite different from those that rely heavily on the response of market forces to macroeconomic government fiscal and monetary policies. We are traveling in a new world while using out-of-date road maps showing the direction to stabilization policies of the past. The routes shown as highways under construction have long since been completed. Some outstanding features of the new routes will not be considered until we have a map that shows the terrain they now traverse.

IMPORTANCE OF LARGE FIRMS IN THE U.S. ECONOMY

How important in the economy are the large firms, which tend to behave in recessions as described in the preceding pages? If the reader, like the writer, has not reviewed data on concentration in the last decade or two, there are some surprises ahead. My purpose here is not to lay the groundwork for proposals to restructure the economy but only to describe the economic world to which policies have relevance and in which they might be effective.

The most global measure of the importance of larger corporations in the economy is provided regularly by the Internal Revenue Service. For example, the largest corporations with assets of $250 million and over — 2,004 in number and only 0.1 percent of the total number of firms — owned nearly two-thirds of all corporate assets.[2] Less than 1 percent of manufacturing firms in the 1970s accounted for more than 85 percent of the assets and profits of all manufacturing firms.[3]

Moreover, despite antitrust activities and the freeing of international trade and investment in the post-World War II period, the largest industrial firms have markedly increased their share of industry's total, however it is measured. Assets of the 200 largest industrial firms rose from 45 to 60 percent of total industrial assets from 1947 to 1968.[4] As might be expected, these 200 firms accounted for almost 55 percent of the mergers and other acquisitions of all large industrial firms in the 1948-76 period.[5] The wave of current mergers and acquisitions presaged an increased share for the 200. The 500 largest industrial firms in 1979 employed 77 percent of workers engaged in manufacturing and mining. The same 500 held about 69 percent of total industrial assets in 1979.[6]

Size, and its growth by acquisition, measures only part of the power of large corporations. The largest 50 firms have interlocking directors on the boards of more than 500 of the 1,000 largest companies.[7] In addition, the largest banks have interlocking directors with the largest firms. Nor does the freeing of international trade and investment and the access of U.S. domestic markets to foreign-based parts of transnational firms afford much promise for relief from domestic concentration. Large firms in the Common Market and Japan, encouraged by their governments (and perhaps partially or wholly owned by them), have been growing ever larger and playing the game by rules that tolerate or encourage cartels that are deemed to operate in the public interest.[8]

The model of the economy that is most relevant for both analysis and policy making is clearly one in which about 500 large firms account for the predominant share of mining and manufacturing in the United States. In most individual industries, eight or fewer companies account for an average of more than half of total sales.[9]

The pattern of concentration in industry might also be expected in finance. Large businesses require large lenders to accommodate them. The largest 50 banks held nearly 60 percent of commercial bank deposits as of December 31, 1979.[10] The 50 largest life insurance companies owned 78 percent of all life insurance assets as of December 31, 1979.[11]

IMPORTANCE OF LARGE UNIONS

Even labor organizations seem to be subject to the pervasive tendency toward concentration. "The 12 largest national unions, with half a million members or more, encompass approximately half of all union members in the country; the other half are distributed among more than 160 national unions."[12] In order of size the largest unions were teamsters; autoworkers; united food workers (before 1979, retail clerks and meatcutters); steelworkers; electricians; machinists; carpenters; laborers; state, county, and municipal service employees; and communications workers. Only 4 of the present 11 largest seem to parallel the size concentration of the industrial structure, a fact that has considerable bearing on the effectiveness of these organizations in the national policy-making process. More important, somewhat less than 30 percent of the labor force is attached to some form of union (including the National Education Association in total membership).

As a countervailing power to big companies, unions have been somewhat overrated. Although steel, aluminum, paper, and paper board workers are 50 to 75 percent organized and automobile workers 75 to 100 percent organized, manufacturing as a whole is only about 50 percent organized and is losing employment in absolute and relative terms. This is also true of coal mining, which has lost ground and like manufacturing is now only about 50 percent organized. Transportation, a largely regulated industry, is almost completely organized.[13]

The foregoing summary of the extent of concentration obviously calls for some analysis of the causes. The antitrust laws have been in effect since 1893, but they have not been applied to concentration per se; mere size is no offense. There must be pervasive forces in the economy that have encouraged concentration despite many years of political and legal efforts to check it.

In the discussion that follows on causes of concentration, I wish to make clear that I am not passing judgment on the question of whether economic efficiency resulting from bigness of companies might be obtainable by means other than size, although in many cases it is difficult to argue otherwise. Large size of business is with us, and still larger size — to a point, at least — seems inescapable. Those who wish to diminish the size and power of large corporations have many ingenious proposals for promoting disintegration and deconcentration. In a later section, I shall discuss some of these proposals. For the present, I wish only to explain some of the influences that have brought us to a business structure in which large firms are of predominant importance.

CAPITAL ACCOUNTING AS A STIMULUS TO CONCENTRATION

In the early 1950s when demand for steel was accelerating because of the Korean War, the New England Council, a regional development group in New England, undertook a serious effort to establish an integrated steel mill in the region on deep tidewater. It anticipated that very large bulk carriers of ore and coal, and new technologies such as oxygen furnaces and continuous casting — all now in common use — would favor such a location. These are the same conditions incorporated in the subsequent rebuilding of the Japanese steel industry, acknowledged in the U.S. trigger price system for steel imports as the lowest-cost such industry in the world today, despite possession of negligible amounts of iron ore and coal.

The promotional effort for an integrated modern steel mill in New England, being carried on by a business group, had friendly relations with U.S. steel companies. To test the feasibility of the proposal, a consulting firm was employed to determine if investment, sales, costs, and profitability would justify establishing the plant to produce about a million tons per year of flat rolled steel. To make the study as practical as possible, cost estimates were derived from the lowest-cost existing plants of Bethlehem Steel, which cooperated with the consultant. While this procedure did not permit testing the newest technology and the lowest-cost sources of some raw materials, it did avoid theoretical estimates. If one can assume good faith all around, the study showed rather conclusively that a newly built plant could not make a competitive rate of return, and the project was shelved. While it is easy to argue that the industry did not want the plant anyway, I believe that for a plant using the low-cost existing technology that was the basis of the estimates, the calculations were not much out of line and illustrate why new producers are reluctant to enter heavy capital-investment industries with new plants. This conclusion is also illustrated by a recent case for which data were disclosed.

The head of a heavy capital-investment industry provided a case study in the 1970s for a chemical material component entering into a widely used bulk chemical product sold in the United States and abroad. In 1968, when the prevailing price of the product was $125 per unit, the company built an economic-size plant to produce it with an investment of $110 million. (All prices have been adjusted by a random number to disguise the source.) When, about ten years later, it completed a duplicate plant, which cost $395 million, the price had advanced to $300 per unit. The new plant was profitable at $300, and the old plant was phenomenally so. Asked why someone else would not build a plant at the $300 price, the executive providing the data replied that a new entrant would lose his shirt when, as he expected, the inflated price would go down. We will survive, he said, because in effect we have a composite investment in two plants; a brand new entrant with only a high-cost plant would go bankrupt. Meanwhile, the company with the composite investment was subjected to an antitrust investigation of the high prices and profits it was obtaining on the blended-capital-cost basis.

The executives engaged in this discussion quickly agreed that what was at fault in such a case was the cost basis for plants used in the accounting, a point earlier demonstrated in Chapter 4. But the wider ramifications as they apply to concentration of industry extend throughout the postwar period of rising plant replacement costs. They go a long way toward explaining why new plants in heavy capital-investment industries have been built mostly by existing companies able to use a composite capital cost and also why plants based on old or obsolete technology are not being replaced more rapidly. These conditions are the product of faulty accounting for depreciation reinforced by faulty tax laws.

The corporate behavior just described may not have been designed as a barrier to the entry of new firms into industries requiring heavy investment in plants and equipment, but in a long period of continuing inflation, and in combination with a pricing policy based on blended capital costs of old and new plants, it was undoubtedly effective as a deterrent to new producers. In terms of the economics of industry, it puts to everlasting shame the contention of most economists who have studied the problem that concentrated industries keep their prices too high through thick and thin. Indeed, while such companies may maintain or even increase their margins over cost in recession, they woefully undercost and underprice their products at other times. The pricing fault of concentrated industries during a long-term inflationary trend is holding prices too low. This practice, accentuated by the tax treatment of depreciation, has resulted in retention of an excessive amount of old high-cost capacity.

REQUIREMENTS FOR ECONOMIC-SIZE PLANTS AS A FACTOR IN CONCENTRATION

The sheer magnitude of capital requirements for economic-size plants in many industries is also a strong deterrent to new entrants. U.S. Steel announced on April 26, 1979, that it was preparing to spend up to $3.5 billion for a new major (four-million-ton) steel mill in the northeast corner of Ohio — an amount that U.S. Steel hesitated to commit and that probably could not be raised by most smaller producers and certainly not by a newcomer. Despite its size, U.S. Steel had not, by the beginning of 1981, begun construction of the proposed plant.

Minimum-economic sizes for some other industries may be cited. The cases were compiled by the author largely because the information was available in published sources, although the estimates are probably too low because of the high rate of inflation since they were made. They are cited only to illustrate how unlikely it would be for a new, untried firm to enter the industry.

For petroleum refining, confined to gasoline and distillate fuel, a plant of 150,000 barrels per day capacity required $300 million in 1974. In 1979 a refinery of 175,000 barrels per day capacity, proposed for Portsmouth, Virginia, was estimated to require $650 million.

For ethylene, a 1.2 billion pound "greenfield" plant called for $600 million in 1977.

For integrated computer systems, over $1 billion was estimated to be required in the early 1970s.

For a two-model automobile plant with a capacity of 500,000 for each model — the minimum size with any prospects — abour $2 billion in the mid-1970s would have been required to go into business. (The Chrysler "bail-out" government loan guarantee alone called for a similar amount.)

Another classic example of the limitation imposed by large capital is offshore oil exploration and exploitation. The cost of front-end money for the rights to explore plus the cost of drilling and the high risk of loss involved require, according to their executives, even the largest oil companies in the world to enter into partnerships in order to bid on federal leases.

ECONOMIES OF SCALE IN PRODUCTION

This is a good place to clarify what is meant by *economies of scale*. The simplest case is illustrated by a fairly unambiguous engineering approach. The current technology and demand for steel, for example, may require that a steel-rolling mill in order to operate at lowest cost must have a capacity to produce a minimum of X million tons per year of sheet-steel products rolled up to Y inches wide. The input of raw materials, their transportation and storage facilities, the facilities for ore reduction and for producing intermediate products such as ingots, and so forth, must be capable of keeping such a mill continuously supplied. The facilities for further processing sheet steel and for storing and transporting it must also be geared to the X-million-ton output. The location of the mill must be such that its total output can be shipped to customers without running up transportation costs to amounts that offset the cost economies of the large-capacity production process. Ideally, the mill would produce a minimum of grades, widths, and thicknesses that would match the market in close proximity, such as automobile and truck body plants and makers of large appliances and containers. The economies of scale just described are based on technology, and any market power that accompanies such a scale of operation is not contrived; it is a natural consequence of the size requirement for the critical unit (the rolling mill) that yields lowest costs.

The frustration of scale economies in industries where firms are large is a never-ending complaint of executives. The recent shutdown of high-cost steel-making facilities in the United States and in France illustrates the problem. Obsolete capacity and high costs forced the U.S. shutdowns, and in one case — Lykes Corporation and Youngstown Sheet and Tube — the Justice Department permitted a merger of the surviving facilities under the "failing business" exception to the antitrust laws. Students of the industry argue that more shutdowns and mergers are necessary to restore the industry's health, but the convenient exception to the antitrust laws has not been available if the take-over was proposed by one of the largest, profitable producers.

Two executives cited similar experience with economies of scale that resulted in each becoming the single surviving producer. One related that in his small market for a chemical product there was room for only one efficient producer, and by technological improvement and the lowering of prices as costs were reduced, his company became the sole survivor. When this resulted, the Federal Trade Commission accused the firm of predatory pricing to keep other people out of the industry and demanded that prices be raised to allow an inefficient producer to enter the industry.

In another case, a widely used mailing device, a single company saw its three or four competitors disappear because they could not compete successfully. In this case, the highly successful surviving firm entered into a consent decree to license patents and provide know-how to potential competitors and in effect to guarantee them a share of the market. The form of competition was preserved at the expense of subsidy by the most successful firm to its competition, but because the largest producer continued to sell most of the volume, the cost was really borne by consumers.

PRODUCT DIFFERENTIATION AS A BARRIER TO NEW COMPETITION

A contrasting type of scale economy occurs in marketing, especially of brand name products sold through retail outlets. A nationwide manufacturer and distributor of a considerable line of grocery products can reinforce brand identity (product differentiation) by national advertising; maintain a large number of warehouses for quick delivery from minimum inventories; run fleets of delivery vehicles, each servicing its whole line of products; and command shelf space in retail outlets for a substantial part of the line because one product helps to sell another to both the retailer and his customers. Manufacturing facilities may have little to do with the economies of scale realized, and technology does not dictate the scale of operations. Most such economies could be obtained by independent warehouse distributors buying from many suppliers, but consumers apparently patronize a well-known brand name because it connotes qualities they prefer. (When during World War II razor blades without brand names on them were distributed through army facilities, there was so much complaint that name brands were restored.)

Theoretical economists have for a half century called attention to the effect of product differentiation as a source of monopolistic power, and executives and marketers have systematically sought to obtain better market control by naming, packaging, advertising, and selling efforts aimed at tying customers to their products. Recent studies of U.S. industries have demonstrated the effectiveness of this technique in discouraging the entry of new competitors. "Empirical studies suggest that for many industries product differentiation represents the major entry barrier. . . . The degree of product differentiation [measured by percent of advertising expenditures to sales] exerted a very substantial positive influence on concentration in the 23-year period 1947-1970."[14]

The product differentiation case is the economist's prime example of needless concentration that may contribute little or nothing to cost efficiency. It does, as we have noted, erect a barrier to the entry of competitors and is under continuous attack by consumer groups. But defensible economies of scale are also applicable to product differentiation concentration: procurement economies from large-scale and steady buying, lower costs of capital because of better credit rating, larger-size short-term borrowing and longer-term security issues, recruitment and retention of more capable executives and employees, and possibly greater use of research and development (R&D).

OTHER INCENTIVES AND BENEFITS RELATED TO SIZE

There are other advantages to size that may not be primary reasons for growth of companies to large size but that occur mainly as a consequence of growth in size.

The first is economies in procurement. These are real savings to suppliers from volume in handling orders, scheduling production, and shipping. These are savings that result from willingness of suppliers to shave prices or perform extra services for volume buyers.

A second economy available to large firms lies in sales management, promotion, and advertising, which, over a period of time, culminates in a brand or reputation preference that is so strong that it provides some insulation against the entry of competitors.

The third economy available to large companies is technological innovation. Companies with 5,000 or more employees account for 80 to 90 percent of private R&D expenditures. In manufacturing such companies account for a share of R&D nearly twice as large as their share of value added. Moreover, more concentrated industries (up to a four-firm concentration ratio of 55 percent) tend to employ more people in R&D per thousand employees than the less concentrated. These data suggest that larger firms, especially those with a large share of the market, can probably afford more R&D and can make it pay off better in new or improved products. In any event, profitability of R&D is higher for large than for small companies.

It may well be that having a large share of the market offers an incentive to develop new products and applications of them for ensuring a volume of sales that will make the R&D investment pay off. A good example is a relatively new subsidiary of IBM, IBM Instruments, Inc., devoted to merchandising, developing, and financing new venture operations for the whole range of the company's equipment. As of 1980 this subsidiary employed 300 persons.[15]

Finally, there may be advantages to size in the attraction, recruitment, and retention of managerial, professional, and highly skilled personnel. Large companies recruit from a wide range of colleges and professional schools and tend to offer the richest package of salary and other benefits. They maintain training and development programs that offer a variety of career tracks. They are to some extent willing to test and improve their selection programs. While there is no way to know whether their managerial, professional, and supervisory people are more able than those of smaller companies, there is one time-tested practice that they can use to achieve results, which is less available to smaller firms: they can employ specialization and division of labor to a greater extent in any function, a practice that is a key to high productivity if the specialized outputs are properly coordinated.

NEW FIRMS AS A CHECK ON CONCENTRATION

There are many who hope and expect that concentration will be reduced by the growth of small companies into bigger ones. But the country's savings are flowing into fewer and fewer hands. The larger banks and investment institutions, the beneficiaries of that trend, tend to be conservative. Pension funds have been subjected to investment standards by the Employee Retirement Income Security Act (ERISA), a needed protection for the employee beneficiaries but a deterrent to pension fund investment in riskier enterprises. Small companies that want to float new securities issues find fewer underwriters to accommodate them and a rising cost of meeting Securities Exchange Commission (SEC) requirements for public issues (in excess of an exemption of $1.5 million). The cost of preparing for required SEC registration for public issues, according to SEC studies, typically ranges between $28,000 and $203,000.[16] The costs of preparing annual and quarterly reports required by the SEC amount to $152 per $100,000 of sales for small companies but only $4 per $100,000 for large ones. These figures are only indicative of the cost burden encountered in meeting the requirements of regulatory and taxing authorities.

Raising capital by borrowing is a relatively more heavily used source of expansion by small companies than by large ones. The mere existence of the prime rate, typically the lowest rate for business loans by banks, is evidence of a persistently lower cost for the most credit-worthy large borrowers. Studies made in the mid-1960s, when interest rates were lower than in recent years, indicate that the cost of borrowed capital to a $1 billion firm was about one percentage point lower than for a $10 million firm. The difference in the 1970s must have been more than twice as much. But more important, larger borrowers tend to obtain a priority on loans. When credit is tight, the smaller firms and higher credit risks are more likely to find the credit well to be dry. Large firms at such times provide credit to smaller suppliers and customers, a commendable practice but one that strengthens the market position of larger firms.

Greater reliance on monetary policy for inflation control has increased the influence of credit as a means of market control for larger firms. High interest rates and tight money as practiced in the 1970s constitute one of the most perverse influences against maintenance of the kind of innovative competitive system that we are relying on, in the longer term, to accelerate productivity improvement. High interest rates and tight money tend to channel credit to the better credit risks. The better credit risks are basically the bigger institutions, the bigger firms. In times of tight money and high interest rates, the smaller, new, growing firms on which we rely to inject innovation and new vigor into the economy are the ones that go to the wall or into the arms of high-cost financiers or bigger firms. The effects of monetary policy as practiced in recent years have yet to be measured in terms of what it does to the structure of the whole economy. I have little doubt that the seesaw of tight and less tight monetary policy is a strong, if unwitting, ally of large firms and a force making for more concentration.

SOME BENEFICIAL EFFECTS OF MERGERS

Take-overs and mergers that add to concentration may provide efficient and effective ways of reallocating capital frozen in obsolete and low-earning companies. Numerous discussions on take-overs with conglomerate makers who use this pattern can be stated in simple economic terms: companies that are locked into obsolete capacity — earning far less than going rates of return on capital and often poorly managed, especially if closely held by families and their trustees — can be considered obstacles to the redeployment of capital into more productive, higher-yielding uses. If acquired by competent entrepreneurial management, their capital can be unfrozen and reinvested in more productive ways. The histories of Textron and other conglomerates supply many examples of this type.

Most economists neglect this process of capital redeployment by take-overs and consider only the bail-out process in which a declining concern or industry is reorganized and subsidized (for example, Conrail and Chrysler) or taken over by government and subsidized (for example, British Steel and U.K. coal mining).

To reorganize and refinance a failing company as a single entity through market processes and bankruptcy is expensive, time-consuming, and often more profitable to attorneys, trustees, bankers, and various other outsiders than to its owners or to the economy. By contrast, redeployment of the capital of a company acquired by a conglomerate (which may increase its concentration ratio for some products as a result of the acquisition) is only an internal administrative matter that may involve replacement of some management personnel, scrapping of some facilities, conversion of others, and sale of viable units that cannot be brought up to as high a level of profits by retention as by sale to other companies. This process in the aggregate adds up to a massive reorganization that transfers capital and other resources to more productive uses if the reorganization is skillfully executed. Sometimes these activities may be dominated by insiders looking for the fast buck, but often they result in more productive use of resources and better careers for most officers and employees. Most people would agree that the processes are necessary in a dynamic economy; most would prefer such actions as take-over and reorganization to company bankruptcies and liquidations. To the extent that they are blocked by law or decree, the economy would probably be worse off.

CONCENTRATION AND THE POWER OF RECIPROCITY

One of the largest New York banks, announcing in 1978 the replacement on its board of directors of several prominent corporate executives who had retired from their corporate positions, explained that outside members on the bank's board must be active executives in their own companies, presumably capable of delivering or retaining business for the bank from their own and other companies.

An executive in the primary metals industry, discussing General Motors's (GM) sales performance a number of years ago, explained an element in that enviable record. If you do business with GM, he said, you must understand their practice of reciprocity. They are our biggest single customer and account for more than a third of our sales. So when we buy automobiles and other automotive products, they insist on reciprocity. To them this means that we buy *all* of our requirements from GM. (In view of subsequent antitrust actions involving other companies and the upgrading of business practices, this example is not meant to reflect current conditions.)

Reciprocity is one of the most pervasive aspects of U.S. business and, probably, an even stronger influence abroad where the largest banks often control or exert some power over a considerable share of large firms. Reciprocity is not per se unlawful, like tie-in sales, because it is based upon a sense of mutual obligation. The practice lowers selling costs and need not impose any extra costs on purchases made by the dominant firm to promote or maintain sales to suppliers. Antitrust cases, consent decrees, and decentralization of management have greatly attenuated the questionable aspects of reciprocity, but it continues to be practiced.

Sears Roebuck has for many years practiced a benign reciprocity that is difficult to fault. Because of its tremendous volume, it has helped to establish and assist producers for many of the products that it sells. Sears's policy of local sourcing makes this especially true for its branches in developing countries. In Brazil, for example, the company literally created manufacturers to supply it, trying never to absorb more than half of a factory's output. The government's economic development ministers literally begged the company to establish more stores in Brazil as instruments of development. Similarly, in periods of credit crunch, as has been noted, large companies have provided or endorsed credit to their suppliers and customers.

Nevertheless, the effect of concentration on reciprocity cannot be ignored. Big sellers are big buyers in whose good graces smaller supplying firms wish to remain. A large customer is actively courted. A large company maintains a kind of benign fiefdom within a semifeudal network of obligations and loyalties, which is to a considerable extent outside the market system. The larger a company becomes, the more prized is the supplier's relationship to it. The main effect is to make it difficult for a new entrant — an interloper — to crack the web of relationships, many of a personal nature, in order to sell to large companies that are already tied to their suppliers by reciprocal sales relationships.

The same kind of network of personal contacts, favors, and obligations has been easily extended to the arena of government. Local managers and officers of large companies know or are expected to know local elected officials; higher-level officers are expected to have the same relationship to higher-level officials; and so on, up to Chief Executive Officers, who are guests at the White House as well as hosts and fellow club members of high government officials. Almost overnight this loose network of business-social-political relationships has been converted into a political force. Elected officials have always used patronage and contracts to strengthen their sinews of power. Large corporations, with incomparably better and more powerful organizations, have – by adding political action committees (PACs) for financing election campaigns, threatening plant shutdowns, or promising expansion of old plants or establishment of new ones – moved a long way toward rivaling or surpassing the power of government on issues that are of special importance to them. The effectiveness of this new force is limited to those issues on which large companies are not themselves in conflict. But there are plenty of those. To the panoply of power inherent in size, reciprocity, and social responsibility a new dimension is rapidly being added: political influence openly and lawfully exercised through PACs and decisions to locate, expand or curtail plant operations.

BUSINESS INTEREST – THE SHADOW AND THE SUBSTANCE

The contrast between the reality of the economic structure and the shadows, symbols, and misconstructions that lurk in the classical traditions of economics has been an unhappily pervasive thesis of this work. The disparity of conceptions is not without consequences that extend far beyond intellectual disputation.

Some business executives may be willing, as Lenin said, to sell revolutionaries the rope with which the sellers will be hanged. Socially responsible business executives, some would say, might even donate the rope. This may seem to be the beginning of a plea to stop supporting causes devoted to social reform – a useless suggestion because most such causes are not supported by business anyway. On the contrary, I shall argue that businesses lean toward supporting most so-called conservative economics without knowing that in so doing they may be providing the rope that could be used to hang the very system they support.

The conservative or classical approach is directed at reducing the encroachment of government on the liberties (and pocketbooks) of the citizens, an encroachment that is alleged to be for the benefit of politicians and the bureaucracy. That encroachment is ostensibly for the purpose of achieving a more just distribution of income and wealth. (Old-fashioned liberals of the nineteenth century breed would quickly ally themselves with the opponents of encroachment; indeed, today's conservative draws most of his philosophy from Adam Smith and his intellectual heirs.)

Minimizing the intrusions of government taxation, regulation, welfare, health care, and other social programs is to argue for a nongovernment private or market solution for the problems that governments have sought to correct. Responsible large businesses can and have set up health insurance and pension plans for employees and might even be able to provide modest private alternatives to government welfare programs. The classicists argue that if government intrusion were less and taxes lower, businesses could invest more, the wages and costs of hiring people would be lower, and the need for social welfare programs would be less. Released from the shackles of government, free markets and voluntary giving might resolve many social problems. If the private enterprise system produces too much, prices will fall; if unemployment becomes a problem, wages will fall; at lower levels of prices and wages demand will more easily clear markets; and so on. It is when this attractively simplistic promise cannot be met that the classical conservative (or traditional liberal) must make explicit the rest of his agenda.

Obviously, if the system does not work as assumed, it is claimed that markets are not free. If prices do not fall when demand slackens, there is not enough competition. If wages do not fall when unemployment rises, unions have fettered labor markets. The power of business firms over prices and of unions over wages must be overcome by breaking up the centers of excess power through vigorous application of antitrust laws and other measures to make markets behave like their theoretical models. Sooner or later, the classical philosophy must be put into practice by programs that will deprive large companies and other major sources of market power of their means of frustrating the (theoretical) workings of the market system. This was the philosophy of the United States in the half century centered on 1900; it still has vigorous supporters in market-sheltered educational and research institutions and in some very large business and financial companies that possess a degree of market power that belies their advocacy. That philosophy either was never adopted or has long since been abandoned by other industrial countries. It is they who would inherit if, in attempting to turn back the clock, we should damage our productive base by breaking up the large institutions that provide the sources of economies of scale and technological progress integrated with mass marketing and finance.

OLIGOPOLISTIC CAPITALISM AND SOCIALISM

It may be useful to add a final methodological disaggregation of the composite of concepts included in the objective: a free enterprise, competitive market price system. The existing system whose characteristics have been described herein can be termed an *oligopolistic system* and its antithesis, the *socialist system* — government control of means of production.

It is interesting to observe in Table 9 that both systems, in some fashion, share affinities for or rejection of key elements in the free enterprise, competitive market price system. While the systems are at loggerheads intellectually, in practice both reject free entry of competitors as a destabilizing influence and both prefer to bring aggregate supply and demand into balance by management of supply and demand rather than by unlimited price movements. Both find that many weak suppliers of inputs is a synergistic condition, but both would opt for "captive" suppliers if necessary to keep them under control. Neither system, however, can reject the only rational approach to an economic allocation of labor and resources and a guide to consumption: market prices. For these functions, both oligopolistic capitalism and theoretical socialism must rely on market-clearing prices, though each uses a different method to establish them.

The really divergent interests of the two systems are displayed when attitudes toward the institutional foundation of a capitalist system are contrasted with those of a socialist. (See Table 10.)

Private decision making and management are basic to an oligopolistic capitalism and cannot be practiced without private ownership of the means of

TABLE 9
Oligopolistic and Socialist Attitudes Toward Elements of Market System

Condition	*Oligopolistic Attitude*		*Socialist Attitude*	
	Favor	*Opposed*	*Favor*	*Opposed*
Free enterprise (easy entry)	No	Yes	No	Yes
Price competition				
Many producers of final products	No	Yes	No	Yes
Many suppliers of labor and other inputs	Yes	No	Yes	No
Market price system (cost-price allocation of resources and goods; freedom of choice to consumers)	Yes	No	Yes (modified by allocation and ration system)	No

Source: Compiled by the author.

TABLE 10
Oligopolistic and Socialist Attitudes Toward Legal Institutions and Government

	Oligopolistic Attitude		*Socialist Attitude*	
Condition	*Favor*	*Opposed*	*Favor*	*Opposed*
Private ownership of means of production and consumption	Yes	No	No	Yes
Private decision making and management (within a system of law)	Yes	No	No	Yes
Government subject to democratic control with free elections	Yes (qualified)	No	No	Yes (qualified)

Source: Compiled by the author.

production. Private ownership is equally indispensable for rational consumption in which disposition of income is guided by prices for goods and services.

There may be some question as to whether either system requires the maintenance of a government subject to democratic control with free elections. After all, most encroachment on private ownership and private decision making has come through the democratic political process; the existence of democratic government has provided a way to give public consent to oligopolistic capitalism, to curb its excesses, and to make it generally acceptable. It has probably, on balance, preserved that system against rejection by drastic or violent reaction when it performed inadequately.

Democratic government has restricted full exercise of the powers inherent in private ownership and private decision making by oligopolies. On the other hand, private ownership of wealth by citizens has made it possible to expose shortcomings and excesses of oligopoly, to give criticism a fair hearing, and to protect the political process from domination by those controlling or exercising the powers of ownership over the means of production. Moreover, private property owned and bequeathed by citizens has supported countless voluntary efforts to ameliorate and overcome deficiencies in the social outcomes of oligopoly that were demeaning the quality of life. I see little or no counterpart to these ameliorative functions in a socialist system except as that system is extolled in a theoretical model — a model that has not been practiced by any industrial society in modern times. Private ownership and democratic government are the dominant characteristics that distinguish our system from that of the socialist world, in practice as well as in principle.

To be sure, this outline of two systems in conflict is elementary, yet it serves to isolate the problems that must be faced in the future evolution of the U.S. economy and society. Can our economy demonstrate superiority with limited freedom of entry for competitors and without much of the vigorous price competition that has been assumed by the theorists and praised (but sparingly practiced with restraint) by big business? Can an economy characterized by oligopoly and democratic government create the policies and institutions needed to remove the double scourges of inflation and recession? And can the real world economy of socially responsible oligopoly meet the requirement of a free society that its government be subject to democratic control by citizens freely exercising their rights of citizenship?

To find answers to such questions, we must examine proposals to establish in the real world the conditions and political structures necessary to make the free enterprise competitive market system work like its theoretical model. And if the system cannot be brought into line with its theoretical counterpart, we must consider other modifications of it to bring its performance up to more acceptable standards. Chapter 8 explores the possibilities.

NOTES

1. See Alfred S. Eichner, ed., *A Guide to Post-Keynesian Economics* (White Plains, N.Y.: M. E. Sharpe, 1979).

2. U.S. Department of Commerce, Bureau of Census, *Statistical Abstract of the United States: 1979*. Based on U.S., Internal Revenue Service, *Statistics of Income, Corporate Income Tax Returns, 1976*.

3. Derived by author and Arthur Rones from Federal Trade Commission, *Quarterly Financial Report for Manufacturing Corporations*, and U.S., Internal Revenue Service, *Statistics of Income*, various years. See also, footnote 4, pp. 11 and 29-31.

Proportions used in the text are deliberately scaled down below the highest that are defensible for particular years. "Less than 1 percent" is fewer than 4,000 firms.

4. Samuel Richardson Reid, *The New Industrial Order* (New York: McGraw-Hill, 1976), p. 12.

5. Derived from U.S. Federal Trade Commission, *Economic Report of Corporate Mergers* (Washington, D.C.: yearly summaries). Mimeographed.

6. "The Fortune Directory of the 500 Largest Industrial Corporations," *Fortune*, May 5, 1980, pp. 274-301 and *Statistical Abstract of the United States*, 1979.

7. Reid, *The New Industrial Order*, p. 38.

8. While including foreign companies or operations in concentration ratios may affect the numbers here, ratios that have meaning in the U.S. market have little meaning when expressed in terms of world markets where the game is played according to different rules. Use of ratios of concentration within the United States provides a measure of domestic corporate power, which is a relevant consideration in this study.

9. The degree of concentration through the range of U.S. manufacturing industries is surprisingly large. In 1970 the top 8 of the largest firms in 292 manufacturing industries (representing 74 percent of value added by all manufacturers) that remained in essentially unchanged classifications accounted for a weighted and unweighted average of 54 percent of sales in their industries, and this average had risen from the level of a dozen years earlier. Even the four-firm average concentration ratio for these industries exceeded 42 percent.

Willard F. Mueller and Larry G. Hamm, "Trends in Industrial Market Concentration, 1947-1970," *Review of Economics and Statistics* 56 (November 1974): pp. 511-520.

10. "The Fortune Directory of the Largest Commercial Banking Companies," *Fortune*, July 14, 1980, pp. 148-149. Total assets, all commercial banks, from *Federal Reserve Bulletin* 66 (1980): p. A16.

11. "The Fortune Directory," ibid., pp. 150-151. Total assets from U.S. Department of Commerce *Survey of Current Business* 60 (March, 1980).

12. John T. Dunlop, "Past and Future Tendencies in American Labor Organizations," *Daedalus*, 107, no. 1 (1978), pp. 79-96.

13. Ronald Berenblim, "The Declining Market for Unionization." New York, The Conference Board, Information Bulletin no. 44, August 1978.

14. Mueller and Hamm, "Trends in Industrial Market Concentration." A similar finding with respect to differentiation as a barrier to entry in Canada was made by Dale Orr, "The Determinants of Entry: A Study of the Canadian Manufacturing Industries," *Review of Economics and Statistics*, February 1974, pp. 58-66.

15. Robert Hutchings, vice-president, IBM Instruments, Inc., personal interview.

16. Judith Miller, *New York Times*, November 5, 1977. Article is based on SEC internal memorandum obtained by a request under the Freedom of Information Act.

8

ROLES OF THE LARGE COMPANY
IN THE REAL U.S. ECONOMY

My primary purpose in most of these pages has been to illuminate how the U.S. economy really works by presenting the facts about the business structure and the policies, both public and private, that executives of large companies consider to be essential for healthy companies and a prosperous economy. By now it should be evident that there exists a hiatus between how the economy really works and the views on that subject implicit in the expressions of many economists and professed spokesmen for business. The latter extol the virtues of free markets and competition implicitly in terms of the operation of an abstract model and the results to be obtained by relying on this intellectual construction to solve almost any problem without real-world government intervention. At the same time, business executives reveal in their private discussions of real-world public policy problems that they often borrow their rhetoric from economists who use the same or similar terms but with different meanings. In considering any specific problem or policy, executives drop the ambiguities and explain and justify their decisions and actions in pragmatic experiential terms.

One economist, in an annoyed castigation of his colleagues, wrote:

> The Land of Perfect Competition, from which the textbooks start, is inhabited entirely by disembodied variables and constants that, though bearing the names of economic phenomena, are devoid of substance. Here demand without demanders, supply without suppliers, capital without capitalists, profit without shareholders, interest without money-lenders, and labor without laborers act and react in complex series whose outcome, if Government and Monopoly are kept at bay, is the maximization of all good things.[1]

THE SPECIAL LANGUAGE OF COMPETITION

A good example of the hiatus is the meaning of *competition*. To the business executive *competition* is rivalry of all kinds: other firms, substitute products, substitute materials, imports, better credit terms, delivery, service, quality, discounts and allowances, warehousing, and the myriad of elements that surround the transaction and that together with the price constitute the buyer's cost. Moreover, each transaction has one foot in the past and one in the future of real time, and company policy embodied in the transaction rests upon consideration of the long-term value of the customer to the firm, the possible effects on constituencies of its treatment, and other effects on the life and growth of the company.

When economists and business executives interchange ideas about policies that are not yet crystallized in the thinking of either, the schizophrenia in their rhetoric is revealed. This is painfully apparent from the discussions in depth recounted in preceding chapters. It is especially apparent in the presuppositions used by the different parties, particularly those about presumed competitive price behavior and profit maximizing. These often misguide groups starting from different presuppositions to propose or support opposing policies, most of which if adopted may prove to be ineffectual or counterproductive. How to avoid such outcomes by improving the intellectual foundations, the participants, and the processes of policy making is the major concern of this chapter.

In considering competition and monopoly power, what must not go unnoticed is that business executives' views for the most part reflect the existence of an economic structure in which large firms predominate, the kind of structure that exists today. That structure has been characterized in passing and described statistically in the preceding chapter. The structure described or implicit in the discussions of executives differs markedly from the working models of the system used by most economists as the foundations of their policy proposals. Because restoring competition is the dominant program of economic reformers and is bitterly opposed by the large companies that would be most affected, this subject will be considered in some detail in the pages that follow.

The working model of the mainstream economists, which becomes their paradigm for policy formulation, is a competitive market system composed of a large number of firms, none so large that it has any significant influence on the prices at which it sells outputs or buys inputs. Monopoly and its more numerous cousins, oligopolies, are treated as special cases in the economists' usual analyses. In fact, the special cases predominate.

Monopolistic deviations from the model are charged with creating suboptimal conditions (compared with those expected from the abstract model of pure competition) in which profits are excessive, prices are higher than they need be (for example, are in excess of marginal variable cost), output is less than could be sustained at lower prices, and consumers can afford to buy less output (because of the monopolistic prices) than could be produced at the

144 / Business Power and Public Policy

minimum (marginal) cost. Thus, it is argued (from the model) that economic resources are not allocated efficiently because in the absence of monopolistic restraints consumers would be able and willing to buy more at the lower prices possible under pure competitive conditions. Moreover, some would add that oligopolistic prices generate excessive profits and therefore excessive salaries and dividend incomes for those in control. This is the theoretical static case (abstracted from real time) against alleged monopolistic behavior without the usual academic trimmings.

To this case a dynamic (cyclical) argument is often added. It is argued by many that the degree of autonomous power over prices exercised by oligopolies permits them to maintain prices (or at least margins over direct cost) in periods when there is a general recession in demand for whatever reason. Instead of cutting prices, which might maintain output and employment when demand drops, it is argued that oligopolists cut output and reduce employment but maintain prices, thus adding to the severity of recessions. This leads to the further charge that such behavior puts a heavier burden on government to adopt compensating fiscal policies — to cut taxes to maintain total demand, to turn on make-work and other government-income maintenance programs, and to adopt expansive monetary policies. It is further argued that the worsening of recessions by oligopolistic behavior stimulates government intervention to prop up the weaker and more competitive parts of the economy — to support farm prices; to subsidize mortgage loans in order to maintain housing construction, to establish small-business credit institutions, and to adopt or tighten up regulations limiting competition in transportation and communications; to restrict imports; and to undertake a myriad of other activities to assist sectors of the economy heavily impacted by a general recession in demand. This cyclical case against monopoly and oligopoly is, of course, unproved; and it is questionable that a downward wage-price spiral in a recession such as that experienced in the early 1930s would either be tolerated or more effective in curing recessions than countercyclical fiscal and monetary policies.

This indictment of oligopoly has led in the last two decades to proposals for remedies to oligopoly far more specific than those contained in the antitrust laws as they have been enforced in the past. These more stringent proposals grew out of three major developments in the last half century. One was the failure of the antitrust program to prevent the progressively greater concentration of firms that has made the very large company the dominant form of business in our economy, if dominance is measured by the proportion of assets, profits, and employment that is controlled by the larger companies. The second was the incorporation into the mainstream of economic doctrine after 1930 of the theory of oligopoly that was described above. The third was appreciation of the enormous power and influence, especially over legislation, of the concentrated industries, power that was deemed also to have too much influence over people's lives.

The preoccupation of mainstream economists with the simplistic pure competition model consisting of many competitive sellers and buyers has become the usually implicit basis for policies on how to restructure the economy to make it more compatible with the theory underlying the model of pure competition. Empirical studies have led many economists to recognize the essentially oligopolistic structure of the economy and to prescribe how it might be reformed to make it behave in closer consonance with the pure competition model, which more nearly resembles their stock in trade. They have had assistance from spokesmen for business who pass over the intellectual dilemma posed by the dominance of oligopoly and argue their case directly from the philosophy of laissez-faire, contending that the market system *as it presently exists* will produce a reasonable approximation of the textbook results.

In fairness to both schools of thought, I am summarizing four approaches of economists, antitrust specialists, and political leaders advised by them on how to restore a more workably competitive economy before proceeding to my own alternative based explicitly on the proposition that something like the present structure is what we shall be living with for a long time. However, it is important for those who have not reviewed recent work on deconcentration to consider relatively new proposals that are designed to restore a competitive economy by translating into policy the theoretical work on oligopoly summarized above. Glib politicians and business executives who are advocates of laissez-faire, when they realize the conditions that their academic and professional friends consider necessary to restore a competitive economy, may be more willing to consider other alternatives, including partnership of private and public power for resolution of problems that neither can achieve without the other.

PROPOSALS FOR DECONCENTRATING THE ECONOMY

Break Up the Largest Firms

One traditional view of how to reduce the excessive market power of large firms is to break them up into smaller units, relying upon an increased number of smaller sellers to increase competition with each other. If economies of scale result in monopolies that cannot be broken up, the traditional approach has been to subject their prices, service, and rates of return on capital to regulation and to rely upon regulation rather than competition to protect the public interest. This alternative, or a take-over by government, puts the problem outside the scope of restoring a competitive economy.

The essence of one approach to deconcentration that is contained in several recent wide-ranging proposals is to use a statistical measure to establish a presumption of oligopoly. The leading indicators of oligopoly are the share of an industry's output controlled by the largest four firms (because those data are available) or the market share of the largest firm (for which data are also obtainable). Adoption of such measures is premised upon the theoretical demonstration, discussed above, that oligopolies will choose monopolistic pricing and output decisions, even without collusion, as part of a profit-maximizing strategy.

I should emphasize that this presumed behavior is based heavily on theoretical rather than empirical demonstrations and calls attention to the vehement denials of executives of oligopolies that they seek to maximize profits.

The rationale of one very reasonable version of the breakup approach is perhaps best illustrated by the recommendations for a Concentrated Industries Act by a White House Task Force on Anti-Trust Policy in 1968.[2]

The proposed Concentrated Industries Act would apply to certain oligopolistic industries in which (a) four or fewer firms have accounted for 70 percent or more of the industry's sales in defined recent years; (b) the identity of the four largest firms has not materially changed in recent years; (c) total industry sales were more than $500 million (1968 dollars) in four of the last five years; but (d) industry sales and market share of the four largest firms are not in substantial decline.

The proposed act calls for the attorney general to bring a proceeding against the oligopolistic group before a proposed Special Anti-Trust Court. If the court makes an affirmative decision, the group would have a year to take voluntary action to reduce concentration to an acceptable level or face court-directed relief aimed at reducing the market share of each such firm to no more than 12 percent.

The Special Anti-Trust Court would also have broad powers to grant relief from oligopolistic industries, including the power to remove or restrict the use of valid patents and contractual arrangements. But in this and other proposals there is a strong injunction against actions that would result in substantial losses of economies of scale. This provision is a very desirable and realistic one that takes account of the possibility that economies of scale may result in oligopoly prices lower than those attainable by a more competitive number of producers.

The proposed Concentrated Industries Act offers a middle-of-the-road, relatively simple, and intelligible set of proposals for deconcentration. It is a logical (but not necessarily desirable) conversion of economic theory (which may be ill-founded) into an antitrust proposal. But it is mechanical and harsh and, worst of all, makes no allowance for the good behavior of socially responsible large firms that do not conform to the theoretical norms of setting excessively high prices to maximize profits. Enforcement of such an act would be inequitable, and, even worse, it would reduce the power of U.S. firms to compete in both domestic and world markets against foreign competitors that are assisted by their governments to grow by merger and many other means in order to be more competitive.

Prohibit Further Growth of Largest Firms by Merger

A second category of proposals accepts the fact of concentration but seeks to put a ceiling on it rather than to break up existing large firms. Senator Edward Kennedy, then chairman of the Senate Judiciary Committee, early in

1979 introduced a bill to this effect with support from the chief of the antitrust division, John Schenefield, and Michael Pertschuk, chairman of the Federal Trade Commission, but without an opinion from the White House except consent for the two highest antitrust officials to testify.

Like the proposed Concentrated Industries Act, which has remained dormant for ten years, the main features of this proposal are simple. The target is mergers or take-overs of large companies by large companies, especially the conglomerate form, which has not been given much attention by antitrust law enforcers. It is directly aimed at preventing the largest companies from growing larger by mergers. The proposed act would prohibit mergers between companies with total assets or annual sales in excess of $2 billion. This provision would affect the top 100 industrial companies.

The bill would also conditionally prohibit mergers between companies with assets or sales of more than $350 million but less than $2 billion or between a company with more than $350 million of sales or assets and another having 20 percent or more of its industry's sales. In either case, for the $350-million-to-$2-billion-size firms, the prohibition would not apply if the firm could prove that merger would enhance competition or result in substantial gains in efficiency or if the acquiring company divested itself of a part of its business equal in size to that gained in the merger. This second part of the proposal would affect another 400 or more companies. Firms in the $350-million-to-$2-billion range could ascertain in advance from the antitrust agencies if one or more of the defenses pertained; if so, the act would not apply. None of the affected firms would be prohibited from growing from within by technological innovations, efficiency, and other sources not depending on mergers. For what it may be worth, this proposal, drastic as it seems, is a reduced version of a more comprehensive stopgap reform proposed 15 years earlier by an antitrust judge.

Like the proposed Concentrated Industries Act, the new proposal establishes a presumption of monopoly power and puts the burden of defense on the accused who is limited to using only two grounds for defense: improved competition (not defined) or increased efficiency. Other forms of good behavior, of which there are many, are not admissible defenses.

The battle against gaining size by merger is obviously an old one, and its failure to make progress is either a tribute to the good behavior and the persuasive case made by large companies or to their power in opposing such legislation, or both.

Limit Company Growth by Taxation

A third category of proposals attempts to discourage size by using the taxing power of the federal government. One leading proposal measures market power by above-average profit rates,[3] and several others give this factor considerable weight. Above-average profits are attributed by statistical analysis to be closely related to high market shares of the largest firms. Remedial measures lean heavily on a tax reform establishing graduated progressive corporate profits taxes. Progressively higher corporate tax rates would be applied on the basis of the market share enjoyed by the company. (The progressive taxes would also be applied to banks that finance concentration as well as to concentrated companies.) The standard rate of corporate profits tax might apply up to a company's average competitive rate of return. To this would be added graduated surtaxes on profits above the competitive rate, based upon broad market share categories. For example, for a company with a market share between 40 and 60 percent, a surtax of 5 percent above the standard tax rate would be applicable to profits in excess of the competitive rate; for a share between 60 and 80 percent, a surtax of 10 percent above the standard rate; and so on.

This type of proposal is cited because it, too, is derived from the same theoretical framework as the more elaborate proposals of the type previously discussed. The taxation approach does not, however, easily accommodate cases in which high market shares and higher-than-competitive profits are based on economies of scale, valid patents, innovations, better management, and other highly defensible causes. Nor does it penalize companies with a very large market share that earn only a competitive rate of profit – the "satisficing" standard. (The relationship between market shares and profit rates is not clearly established and is debatable; many companies having large market shares earn only modest rates of profit or less.)

Reduce Bigness by Encouraging New Competitors

A fourth general category of proposals for restoring a competitive economy is based on the principle of increasing the number of competitors by encouraging their growth or removing obstacles to it. It would outlaw or weaken what are perceived to be impediments to entry of competitors, encourage new competitors, and eliminate restrictive practices. Because the list of such incentives and obstacles to new competition is almost without limit, a sample of leading examples will convey the nature and intent of the approach proposed. Most of these proposals are presented here for illustration but with evaluation left largely to the reader.

1. Lessen restrictions on imports – not simply by lowering tariffs but by reducing nontariff barriers like grading and labeling (to the importing country's standards), lengthy inspections, conflicting valuations for tariff purposes, state and local government standards of quality in excess of national standards of quality, and especially a requirement by local governments of domestic sources for their own government purchases. The anticompetitive measures just identified already have wide opposition, and some progress has been made toward reducing them in the 1979 legislation ratifying the last General Agreement on Tariffs and Trade (GATT) agreements. In this area of trade restrictions, the United States has probably sinned less than it was sinned against.

2. Ensure supplies of raw materials to new competitors — minerals, forest products, fuels, and so on — where adequate sources of supply at reasonable costs are not ensured but are necessary for financing and continuous process operations. This may require nationalization or compulsory sharing of domestic sources of some raw materials, compulsory sharing of foreign sources, and a requirement that resources owned by large companies be subject to long-term contracts with new competitors.

3. Lessen patent barriers to new competitors by government financial or other assistance to new firms for legal action challenging the validity of patents, shortening terms for which patents are valid, or requiring licensing on reasonable terms — if necessary on terms set by government. Some of these recourses are probably already available through the courts to both government and private complainants.

4. Abolish the right of sellers to choose their customers as long as the customers are financially sound.

5. Provide for early vesting of pension and retirement rights of key employees and eliminate provisions in employment contracts that prevent early retirees from working for competitors after leaving a company to encourage responsible people in existing firms to establish new competitive firms.

6. Allow or encourage mergers by smaller competitors where an industry is dominated by one or two large producers, especially if the smaller firms can introduce innovations. Establish an investment bank to finance such mergers if private sources are unwilling to do so.

7. Extend the government's preferential buying system now accorded to small businesses to new firms of larger size in oligopolistic industries.

8. Outlaw joint ventures of large companies in oil and gas pipelines. Pipelines already jointly owned could be made common carriers.

9. Eliminate the power of independent regulatory commissions to restrict entry and/or set rates in industries that have prospects of being workably competitive — for example, trucking, air transportation, broadcasting, and other communications. There has been considerable movement in these directions.

10. Outlaw rate setting by private conferences and associations. Examples are legal fees set by bar associations and ocean freight rates negotiated by conferences of carriers.

11. Establish public corporations to provide "yardsticks" of costs and services in some industries that have shown persistent high concentration.

12. Eliminate government support for union market rigging beyond the scope of labor union organization and collective bargaining rights. Examples are the Bacon-Davis Act, which often calls for excessive wage rates on government construction. Eliminate overspecific building codes and inspections supported and often enforced by unions that give preference to products of one or a very few producers.

These examples by no means exhaust the list, but they give notice of some things that economists have in mind when they advocate structural changes to improve competition.

Obviously, the foregoing proposals indicate that a great many learned and thoughtful students of the U.S. economy, most of them devoted to a private competitive market system, have been deeply disturbed by the growing power of a relatively small number of large companies. They fear the effect of the dominance of such companies on the sources and uses of power, the failure of prices to reflect market conditions, the possible deterioration of efficiency in some cases, a slowdown of innovation, and other alleged undesirable consequences of large size. But most are also disturbed about the possibility that deconcentration would reduce economies of scale and have other undesirable side effects. Nevertheless, they are willing to take the risks of more restraint in the short run in order to foster a future return to a state of greater self-regulation through market forces with diminished government regulation or court restructuring.

Clearly, the four categories of reform directed toward restructuring the largest companies have few, if any, supporters among the executives who run them. Yet aside from embracing some enlightened views about corporate social responsibility, the executive corps has been singularly quiet on the question of restructuring companies and company functions in ways that would blunt or deflect the attacks on their size and power. The ideology encompassed in their public speeches and statements is often patently out of date and self-serving. It is based too often on a nostalgic hankering back to laissez-faire but under conditions that Adam Smith would find it difficult and probably impossible to reconcile with his philosophy, which did not encompass much danger of large private industrial corporations dominating a free market.

This is the place to remind ourselves of the distinguished political scientist's earlier characterization of the large corporation as a sovereign body existing only because of the consent of society. When that sanction is accorded, in fact or by law, because of the benefits that it confers on society, the large corporation becomes a piece of government. This is the real character of the large companies that constitute a major part of the economic base of this country, a nation that still contains the greatest concentration of economic power in the world. In the real economy, where large companies are unrecognized parts of government, we must consider how such companies are governed and how they relate to the political structure within which they move and exercise their enormous capacity. Even to frame the subject in this way is to open doors that have long remained closed.

GOVERNMENT-BUSINESS COOPERATION TO MEET NATIONAL NEEDS

The structure of the private economy capable of meeting the needs of the United States is not simply a set of economic arrangments governed by a market system, much as that may be implied in popular ideology. The integration of business power and capabilities with those of government is indispensable for achievement of both government and private goals.

Previous chapters have considered some of the wide range of domestic problems calling for cooperative public-private programs. The most important of these is providing the sinews of national security. Construction of facilities, manufacture of weapons, and, most important, technological and scientific research and development are largely contracted out by government to private companies and institutions, both profit and nonprofit. Government is reasonably efficient in collecting taxes and paying out money but has a questionable record in producing and delivering goods and services of the types that can be contracted out to private (profit or nonprofit) organizations.

Another national macroeconomic problem is an adequate rate of growth, most of which is expected to occur in the private sector and is heavily dependent on private investment. Developing new sources of energy is the latest challenge in this field. The government will not mine the coal, nor is it likely to build full-scale synthetic fuel plants, but it must induce private companies to do such jobs.

High employment, another national objective, can be achieved or sustained mainly by private employers if only for the reason that they employ 80 percent of the labor force. But government-provided incentives are usually necessary to secure enough private cooperation.

The continuing number-one problem, control of inflation, depends very much on what prices and wages are set in the private sector. (Wage increases in the federal government have in recent years been below the guidelines.) Whether the supplement to monetary and fiscal policies is voluntary guidelines or real wage insurance or something else, it is how private sector employers and unions play their roles that will make or break the program. The related problem of international balance-of-payments equilibrium depends heavily on private exports and investment.

Involving less clear-cut issues but still heavily dependent on private sector cooperation with government "carrots or sticks" are problems such as unequal employment opportunity, a national welfare system, training and jobs for the disadvantaged, a comprehensive health care system, and resolution of the most difficult parts of the problem of resuscitating decaying urban areas. The most intractable problems, at least in executives' discussions, are the microeconomic and social issues of social responsibility, reform of the tax system, relations with adversary private organizations (for example, unions), and the government regulation of business, especially to reduce pollution, preserve the environment, and provide safe working conditions. Business leadership in proposing effective programs in these areas has been tardy and often negative.

From the standpoint of national purposes, the foregoing citation of domestic issues for which the public and private sectors share responsibility is but part of the whole. International goals and purposes, although they cut across domestic objectives, may be even more important than the latter. In a worldwide schism between the predominantly private industrial democracies and the socialist and quasi-religious socialist states, the private sectors of the industrialized democracies become, whether they like it or not, the indispensable allies of governments and even combinations of governments — for example, the North Atlantic Treaty Organization (NATO) and the International Energy Agency. The industrial democracies are similarly dependent upon private capabilities in trade, finance, and resource acquisition to match the monolithic power of socialized rival powers, of which the greatest is, for the foreseeable future, the Soviet Union.

The developing countries, mostly dominated by authoritarian socialist, religious-socialist, or military regimes, seek development assistance from, and even mold their civilization on, patterns of the developed countries that have the greatest appeal to them. The national interests of the industrial democracies in these countries are partly humanitarian and partly political. Anastas Mikoyan's son once called on me and asked why a group of business executives should be actively promoting the development of the developing countries. When I answered that one important reason was to keep the Soviets out, he replied that the Soviet Union also had such a reason: to keep us out.

In a world having two superpowers, the United States and the Soviet Union, each related to lesser powers in its camp, to consider that the long-term interests of the United States would be best served by a relentless movement to restore at home and to insist abroad that national economic structures be guided by the mythology of laissez-faire is to court national suicide. National interest and national purposes demand, ideology to the contrary notwithstanding, that the strength of the nation be built upon the demonstrated capacities of its economic components and that government, business, and other institutions fit themselves together to accomplish not only the goals of individual and institutional well-being but the common goals of the nation.

THE GOVERNANCE OF LARGE CORPORATIONS

If large corporations are indeed pieces of government, both in their legitimacy and in many of their functions, they have so far failed to reflect this in their own system of governance. This is a correctable failing recognized by many corporate leaders, but it remains an unresolved problem obfuscated and obscured by the traditional adversary relationship with government that stems in no small part from an ideology nourished by the frontier ethic of bygone decades.

The governance of corporations has traditionally been considered from the standpoint of meeting legal obligations to stockholders, the chartering state, and the Securities Exchange Commission (SEC). If, as this book argues, the large, publicly owned, professionally managed company is, among other things, a piece of government, then the selection, composition, and powers of its governing board of directors are matters of prime public interest. But, as we have seen in the discussion of social responsibilities of large companies, the interface of the company with government is but one of its several relationships with constituencies, not all of them of equal importance. The character and composition of the board must be able to serve all corporate purposes, not simply its money-making function. For the private-public partnership envisioned here, the adequacy and credibility of governing boards are critical questions.

The first and paramount purpose of the large corporation, as it is for most businesses, is to survive and grow as a result of its economic performance: good management, efficient production, growing sales, and satisfactory cost-price relations, all coming down to a bottom line of profits adequate to retain and attract capital. Without reasonable profitability, the necessary cooperation among corporate constituencies becomes frustrated, conflicts cannot be resolved, and decline and decay become a threat. (As the Chrysler case demonstrated in 1979 and the Lockheed case demonstrated earlier, more than loss of jobs and investment are involved in decline and decay. Both companies are important defense contractors, and both are very large employers that cannot easily be replaced in areas where they operate.)

In the U.S. economy in the last quarter of the twentieth century, a second corporate purpose of large companies would usually be to optimize its social performance – to achieve an optimum balance of benefits to the corporate constituencies previously discussed. For many companies heavily dependent on governments for sales, technical assistance, and regulation, one such constituency would have to be the governments in the countries important to its business.

Another corporate objective would be good government-business relations and a favorable political climate at home. This category includes the character and philosophy of elected officials, the attitudes and policies of government toward business in matters of antitrust, taxation, regulation, and the like. While there is an overlap of this function with social responsibility, the great difference between the two is the degree of power and independence that the company can exercise – very much in the case of social responsibility but mostly a subordinate role in its relations with its national government. Indeed, except for other large companies in the same or related lines, the only real challenge to the power of large corporations is governments that have sovereign powers to tax, regulate, and set the terms and conditions with which companies must conform. Dissatisfied constituencies of companies can and do turn to government for redress of company shortcomings.

As a recent Arden House report cogently observes, "The corporation is now perceived as a social unit also having, like other basic social entities (family and school, church and state), responsibilities that transcend economics."[4] This report (and the statement on the role and composition of the boards proposed by the Business Roundtable),[5] addresses by the chairman of the SEC, and recent investigations by congressional committees stem primarily from the disclosure of corporate misbehavior in making illegal campaign contributions and questionable payments abroad to foreign governments, their officials, and peddlers of influence – behavior usually neither known to nor authorized by the relevant boards of the companies involved. These experiences have stimulated proposals for more desirable and responsible composition and roles of boards of directors. But most of the proposals for reform of corporate governance have not carefully considered how either governing boards or the corporations that they govern can best perform their policy-making and other roles in formulating or reacting to home-government programs, policies, and actions or to the utilization of company-related political action committees (PACs) and company personnel and influence in furthering corporate and national interests. There is a commendable amount of relevance to these subjects in the new proposals for reforming the selection, composition, and roles of governing boards.

Traditionally, inside and quasi-inside directors (persons like lawyers and bankers who are "suppliers") have dominated the boards of large companies. A most drastic proposal by Harold Williams, former chairman of the SEC, calls for all but one, and he not the chief executive, to be independent outside directors. Another, that of the Business Roundtable, proposes that a majority be outside directors but that the chairman of the board be the company's chief executive. It must be noted, however, that quasi-inside directors are classified as outside directors in the Roundtable's proposal. The Arden House report proposes that a majority of directors be independent outsiders not in a supplier relationship.

The drastic nature of the proposal that boards contain only one insider and no quasi insiders is illustrated by a survey of the 100 largest industrial companies.[6] To meet this test, 781 of 1,491 directors, or more than half of the directors of the largest 100 companies, would have to be replaced. An even larger proportion of directors of the smaller companies would fail to meet the proposed standard.

The leading proposals also call for nominating committees – for new directors and the chief executive – to be composed entirely or in the majority of outside directors.

It should be noted in passing that these and other recent proposals for changes in board composition implicitly assume that stockholder ratification of changes would be forthcoming if managements propose them. This is a realistic assumption. Institutional ownership or control of stock is common for large companies, and experience demonstrates that in most cases management proposals are ratified by the stockholders. Such changes in board composition as are contained in the more moderate of these proposals might well modify the finding of the Arden House report that "corporate boards are perceived as remote, insensitive, and not reflective of the publics they serve."[7]

While these recent proposals call for greater concern about social problems, they do not explicitly face up to the question of how the board and management should organize to relate more effectively to government to further the company's purposes and the public interest. A board could hardly discharge its responsibility if it did not devote discerning attention to studying forms and levels of taxation, determining the costs and effectiveness of protecting the environment, complying with (or exceeding) health and safety requirements, supporting an effective energy program, conforming to or appealing for exceptions to price and wage guidelines, investing in countries violating human rights by legislated racial or religious discrimination, considering reform of antitrust and consumer protection laws, and examining relations with local and state governments in places where plants are reducing or expanding employment. Policies toward issues such as those just noted demand not only the attention of top management but of a board committee and the full board. If large companies are to play the role of which they are capable in promoting sound and effective government policies, consideration of such policies should be high on the agenda of those who would reform the governance of large companies. It is a subject that has no such priority now, either among those who would reform boards or most of those who presently sit on them.

When the large corporation is conceived to be a piece of government, its own governance should be evaluated in terms of that conception. This political analogy has been neglected in the leading proposals for reforming boards.

There is apparently little disagreement that boards should have a nominating committee made up of a majority, or wholly, of outside directors. The committee should be charged with providing for succession of the top officers and board members. However, except for some concern about a retirement age, there is little evidence that a fixed limit on length of directors' service is considered to be appropriate. There are some good reasons for limiting terms, at least for outside directors. It is assumed that inside directors are already subject to informal term limits related to their tenure in corporate office and the wishes of the chief executive. Without a limit on the period of service, much of the value of outside directors will diminish as directors become members of the team and increasingly responsive to the chief executive and mindful of the fees and emoluments of office.

There is obviously no magic limit for terms of directors, and there should be scope for diversity. There is somethng to be said for a limit of two four-year terms, a practice embedded in the Constitution for the president of the country. If terms ended in years following presidential elections, a large number of good potential (and past) directors would be relinquishing government office and would be able to bring recent relevant experience and current knowledge to corporate boards. And some outgoing directors might become available for service in government.

The piece-of-government concept also calls for consideration of another political analogy. the number of board members. It must be large enough to provide a diversity of talents and to constitute the required working committees but small enough to permit reasonably expeditious decision making. Boards of large companies of ten or fewer members, containing fewer than five outsiders, would hardly inspire public confidence. Large boards of 40 or 50 would be so unwieldy that an executive committee would be the real decision-making body.

The maximum size is a matter that might be left to the discretion of the company's chief executive and nominating committee, but in time and after careful consideration of functions to be performed, a company should be able to define a range for optimum size.

The political analogy might also be applied to nominations for the board. The Business Roundtable has suggested that the SEC review its rules to permit shareholders to propose amendments to corporate bylaws that would provide for share-owner nominations of candidates for board membership. It is not clear whether this would permit friendly but nevertheless contested elections for outside directors, but the possibility of establishing a quota of positions for nominees of shareholders holding a qualifying amount of stock might be analogous to preference primary elections in government. Adoption of any form of this proposal would give additional emphasis to the need to establish a limit to the tenure of outside directors; some well-known personalities could be reelected indefinitely.

All of the foregoing discussion of reform of corporate boards is in keeping with the position of power enjoyed by large corporations and with the need to enhance public confidence in corporate leadership. But it has far greater significance, especially for large companies. It has been emphasized earlier in these pages that large companies exist by reason of a tacit social contract under which the company's benefits to society justify society's consent to the continuance of its size and power. This relationship, tenuous and implicit as it may be, is the most powerful defense against adoption of proposals for wholesale deconcentration like those discussed earlier. The relationship would be enormously enhanced if board majorities of outside directors could be considered to be oversight committees concerned not only with the company's economic performance but equally with how the company carries out its part of the social contract. The company's stature in most cases would be enhanced if, with the strong supporting assistance of its directors and the invitation of government, it played a larger role in formulating public economic and social policies and if those policies were more capable of meeting their objectives.

PRIVATE POWER PARTNERSHIP IN NATIONAL POLICY DEVELOPMENT AND IMPLEMENTATION

In July 1979 President Jimmy Carter invited 130 Americans not in his administration to confer with him at Camp David preceding his addresses to the nation that outlined the administration's energy program. Of these conferees, according to information made public, four were top business executives, four were leaders in finance, and eight were labor leaders. Only one was an executive of an energy company. The combined number of leaders in business and finance, as well as the number of labor leaders, was exceeded by the number of academics — ten — and the number of religious leaders — nine. As far as we know, these meetings were not devoted solely or primarily to energy, but they occurred after cancellation of an address on that subject and were followed by the presentation of the president's energy program. And it must be noted that public acceptance of that program, when a large majority of citizens did not even believe that there was an energy shortage, called for consultation with a wide spectrum of respected citizen leaders.

Perhaps a more dramatic example of the point I am making is illustrated by the concoction of Secretary Schlesinger's abortive energy proposals earlier in the year. According to the media reports, these proposals were drawn up in secret, under tight security, and the names of the participants and their roles were not published, although it appears that they were predominantly from the executive branch. One notably outspoken oil industry executive, John F. Swearingen, cheif executive of Standard Oil of Indiana, summed up the process: "It's a one-way street. By that I mean I can write letters and get no replies. And the President has not seen fit to call in people from the oil industry and seek their advice."[8]

The companies and organizations that control the bulk of the country's wealth not only have a major stake in the government's economic policies, but they are relatively few in number and therefore can easily be consulted. To summarize from the last chapter:

The 500 largest industrial companies employ 77 percent of the industrial workers and control 69 percent of industrial assets.

The 50 largest banks hold 60 percent of the bank deposits, and the 50 largest life insurance companies have 78 percent of all life insurance assets.

The 12 largest labor unions encompass half of the union members in the country.

To illustrate the small number being considered, one auditorium of modest size would hold the leaders of these organizations (although we would not expect that they would ever be called together). A group of that size, if they were in general agreement about it, could largely determine the success or failure of any major government economic program. And, as I have noted earlier, enough of the nation's economy was contained in about 3,000 communities to devise and carry out plans for employment that had a large influence in bringing the country out of World War II, our biggest war, without a postwar depression despite learned advice that such a depression had a predictably high probability.

I am not suggesting that a few hundred executives of private interest organizations become a fourth branch of government or that economic policy making be turned over to such an unauthorized body. I am arguing that in such matters as making national economic policy the traditional adversary relationship between big business and government deprives the country of counsel and support from corporate, labor, and other private sector leaders who could greatly improve the policy-making process, the policies that result from it, and their adoption and implementation.

This is neither a novel nor an unprecedented idea. European and Japanese governments customarily consult with leading economic groups in framing national plans and policies, although liberal and labor governments do less than conservative or middle-of-the-road governments.

The process of informal consultation between leaders of the business sector and government ministers in Western Europe and Japan is facilitated by the comprehensive vertical structure of industrial representation groups such as the Federation of German Industry, the Patronat in France, and Keidanren in Japan. These are organizations composed of the organizations of various sectors of industry, each analogous to a holding company with a top governing board selected by its subsidiaries. The top organizations are headed by career executives with strong personalities and considerable prestige. In contrast, the business organizations in the United States are structured horizontally, having a diverse membership of individuals, companies, and associations organized on a state and local basis.

The proliferation and dispersion of organizations representing economic interests in the United States reflect the structure of our government much more than the structure of the U.S. economy dominated by large national and transnational companies. Whereas parliamentary governments in Western Europe and Japan combine the national executive and legislative powers, in the United States they are separated by rigid constitutional barriers. Our state governments exercise a vast range of powers and functions not subject to central government control as are subsidiary governments of the other large industrial democracies. Our economic interest groups must divide their efforts among the many federal, state, and local government units and further divide their efforts between the federal executive and legislative jurisdictions. While these numbers have a somewhat ambiguous meaning, there are about 40,000 significant units of government in the United States. In this framework, our private economic organizations customarily do a better job of blocking or modifying government policies than generating better ones.

The contrast between the division and fragmentation of governments in the United States and the concentration of private economic power underscores the need for the U.S. government to engage leaders commanding large aggregations of private power in national policy making. Because of concentration of private power, leaders of only a relatively small number of business organizations can be consulted and can participate with counterparts in government in the making of national economic policies and in pretesting their effectiveness as applied to a major part of the economy, which they control or greatly influence.

One of the greatest contributions that executives of large companies can make is uniting national policies with the organization and management of programs to carry them out. The capacity of large companies in this respect is transferable when people in business and in government can work as partners instead of, as is usually the case, as antagonists. Provision for the incorporation of these management capacities into policy making would be one of the major achievements to be expected from a significant contribution to policy making from the corporate side. Government and academic policy makers usually neglect the problems of organization and management implicit in their proposals, often suggesting new independent or emergency agencies, which must later be painfully dismantled and placed in the ongoing structure of government.

Students of politics may, at this point, consider the basic elements of the proposals for partnership in policy making to be naive. Important elements of the economy, to say nothing of the country, appear not to be included in it — farming, small business, minorities, women, environmentalists, not even philanthropy and the rest of the third sector. Such exclusions need not occur. But participation of these groups can be obtained only by representation of the large numbers involved by their chosen leaders. The critics should recall that the 600+ group referred to above is not a political body but merely a counting up of the major sources of economic power that are, as has been explained earlier, inherently a piece of government; that it is proposed only that the 600+ group and representatives from other sectors work together with their government counterparts to develop effective economic policies; and that any proposals that they make would be subject to the usual political process in which all parties participate. It should be emphasized that members of the 600+ are chosen because size and influence make their institutions an unrecognized part of government. Representatives of the large number of smaller enterprises in farming, trade, and a multitude of small enterprises could be represented, but their economic power and influence could not match that of the 600+.

President John Kennedy early in his term met with representatives of several business organizations, presumably to improve relations with them. His opening statement was direct and undiplomatic. He said that business organizations in the name of their large memberships often opposed policies that his administration wished to have adopted. He expressed doubt that the purported opposition really represented the views of the organizations' memberships because he had talked to many members of them and found them to be at odds with the organizations' positions. Turning to Marion Folsom (a former chairman of the Committee for Economic Development [CED] and former secretary of the Department of Health, Education and Welfare) and me, he added that he knew that what he had just said did not apply to the CED because its statements were voted by the people whose names appeared on them, together with their reservations and objections. This episode illustrates the difference between the functions of large membership organizations for representation of business interests and the role of a number of executives of large companies called upon as a part of the economic government to help the duly constituted elected government develop workable national economic policies.

HOW PRIVATE POWER LEADERSHIP CAN BE MOBILIZED

It should not be inferred that all of the 600+ are needed for developing major economic policies. The president in consultation with such assistants as he might wish could use the 600+ group as a panel from which, after appropriate soundings, a small policy group could be chosen. Ordinary prudence dictates that persons having a direct private interest in the policy area should constitute no more than a small minority of such a group. And all members from the private sector should be enjoined to advise only in their personal capacity and guided by their perception of what is in the public interest. To this outside group would be added a select group of knowledgeable and responsible government executive branch leaders.[9] The private-public policy groups could be assisted by career people such as those in the new Senior Executive Service. In the present practice (and law) governing such activities, the final position of the policy group should eventually be made public. If the use of such groups becomes common, the relevant committees of Congress would insist on public disclosure of their advice, a step that could facilitate adoption of their views and recommendations.

A proposal of this type calls for more elaboration than it has been given. A good example of how effective policies can be devised in a major policy area by a group that is in microcosm similar to that proposed here was the (Williams) Commission on International Trade and Investment established by President Richard Nixon in May 1970 and reporting in July 1971.[10] Of its 27 members, 15 were business executives, 2 were from labor organizations, 2 were from financial institutions, 1 was from agriculture, 6 were academic, and 1 was unclassified. It had as advisers key people from the relevant executive departments and agencies who expressed themselves freely but did not take responsibility for the recommendations. Its recommendations led to preservation and enlargement of liberalizing policies for international trade and investment and also prepared the way for the unprecedented dollar devaluation that occurred a few months after the issuance of its report.

How could policy groups including members from the 600+ make a difference in policy formation? One example of an important but little-known need is for firming up the business investment and foreign trade components of the GNP estimates used in making federal government budget projections that must be presented annually to Congress and that constitute the basis for stabilizing fiscal policies. A key element in such projections is firmly committed plans for investment in plants, equipment, and inventory as well as commitments for sales financing and exports. While much of such information is collected by the Commerce Department and private research agencies, little or no effort is made to find out how flexible such plans are and how to induce the 600+ to modify plans in ways that would ease pressure on the federal budget. If the need for economic stabilization calls for a budget deficit, the amount of the deficit appropriate for stabilization can be reduced if corporate investment and exports can be expanded and speeded up. Obstacles to attainment of new private goals could be defined, ways might be devised to remove them, and the national budget deficit might be reduced or eliminated in the next and later fiscal years.[11]

THE CHALLENGE OF CONTROLLING INFLATION

Probably the most important use of a select group from the 600+ would be to help devise a comprehensive antiinflation policy that contained enough weapons to be effective. The Ford administration tried a circuslike mass meeting of short duration that accomplished nothing but a demonstration of confusion and conflicting views. President Carter and his assistants made some imaginative proposals for supplementing monetary and fiscal policies with voluntary wage and price guidelines and a real wage guarantee that did not receive serious congressional consideration.

If any problem requires mobilization of government and private power, it is a viable antiinflation program that can be made to work. So far, the wielders of private power have been asked only for cooperation with antiinflation plans that they had little or no role in devising. And up to now, the government-originated plans have been less than effective (if not a failure).

For a decade the economy has been debilitated and its future threatened by inflation accentuated by successive energy cost increases and other shocks that contributed to a continuing wage-price spiral. Consequences of inflation and of antiinflation measures have included erosion of the country's capital base, declining productivity growth, and seemingly uncontrollable increases in government expenditures to mitigate unemployment, create jobs for the hard to employ, maintain incomes of the poor and the elderly, and provide relief for depressed areas and industries. Fiscal policy, a major antiinflation instrument, has become largely ineffective and will have difficulty even to accommodate selective tax reductions to stimulate investment. The main burden of antiinflation control has fallen on monetary policy, which has slowed down the economy by generating recessions that have emasculated the stabilizing function of fiscal policy and the productivity-increasing role of private investment without much effect on inflation. There has probably never been so much passionate disagreement among the experts both in diagnosis and prescription for a major sickness of the economy.

The characterization of antiinflation measures in the preceding paragraph makes putative solutions part of the problem. Never have leaders in government needed more to join with leaders in the private sector to evaluate the effects of policies that have failed and those in place, to reevaluate their efforts, and to make a fresh start on a private-public program that corrects past mistakes, overrides unattainable political promises, and sets the economy on a course that will show visible progress toward reduced inflation and lessened need for government social expenditures. Without a joining of the understanding and powers of the strategic elements in the private economy with those of the government, there can be little hope for any early success in the antiinflation effort.

The framing of effective economic policies is a shared responsibility of private and public power. It calls for continuous and dedicated effort on both sides and, in particular, for private sector leaders to base their advice upon an objective view of the public interest. That effort should be accompanied by reform of the governance of large corporations (and other organizations) to improve their credibility and to support the First Amendment rights of corporate executives called upon to advise their government. New techniques and capabilities will be required of high-level managers in both business and government. If the suggested reform in policy making becomes embedded in the policy-making process, it would constitute a quiet, evolutionary modification of the Constitution, bringing it into harmony with the real structure of the economy and the needs of the nation.

Failure to institute such reform in the policy-making process in the direction of partnership between private and government power entails considerable risk. The adversary relationship between the two would be continued – but with the tilt toward more private influence on government accelerating if present trends continue. The weight of the countervailing power of labor and public interest organizations is under increasing pressure from corporations and other powerful private organizations pursuing their own private goals. Assigned, often unwillingly, to the role of adversary to government in a kind of civil war, the great aggregates of private power will be forced to try to neutralize or defeat their government opponents. In the fight to win, they will often overkill; desirable parts of measures that might be acceptable to the adversaries will be obliterated along with the most objectionable parts.

Thus, the real loser in the traditional adversary process often will be essential policies that advance the public interest and along with that, piece by piece, our prestige and power as a nation.

NOTES

1. Guy Routh, "The Mist in Economics," *New York Times*, November 8, 1977.

2. A good analysis of this proposal of the so-called Neal Committee, of the Kaysen-Turner proposal, and of the Hart Bill and other proposals is contained in Harvey J. Goldschmit, H. Michael Mann, and J. Fred Weston, eds., *Industrial Concentration: The New Learning* (Boston: Little, Brown, 1974), especially chap. 7.

3. William G. Shepherd, *The Treatment of Market Power* (New York: Columbia University Press, 1975).

4. "The Ethics of Corporate Conduct" (Report of the Fifty-Second American Assembly, New York, Columbia University, April 14-17, 1977).

5. The Business Roundtable, *The Role and Composition of the Board of Directors of the Large Publicly Held Corporation* (New York: Business Roundtable, January 1978).

6. Thomas J. Neff, Board of Directors Composition, Fortune 100 Industrials, Spencer Stuart and Associates, N.Y., September 1978. Mimeographed.

7. "The Ethics of Corporate Conduct," p. 5.

8. Associated Press, interview in Bucharest, Rumania, September 12, 1979.

9. Some are likely to suggest that there is an alternative or supplement to this proposal that takes the form of bringing together members of the executive and legislative branches for policy making, something that is not the practice now and that is the source of constant conflict. An attempt of this type was made by President Dwight D. Eisenhower and Congress in setting up the (Randall) Commission on Foreign Economic Policy in 1954. It was composed of five senators and five representatives (including majority and minority members of the principal committees having jurisdiction over the subject matter) and five private citizens (four business executives and one professor). It was vigorously argued by one of the senior congressional members that the whole process was unconstitutional because those members who were chairmen of congressional committees, who expected to hold hearings and report legislation on the subjects under study, were being asked to commit themselves in advance of the constitutional process by which legislation is generated. For the most part, the congressional members reiterated positions taken by their committees in the past. Our experience in this episode led Clarence Randall and me to exchange vows to oppose for life any repetition of the mixed legislative and public commission as a means for policy making in government, and despite subsequent proposals for such mixed commission, to my knowledge, none of importance has been used since.

10. Report to the President submitted by the Commission on International Trade and Investment Policy, *United States Economic Policy in an Interdependent World*, Washington, D.C.: July, 1971.

11. A quite successful example of forecasting that uses a sample of about 40 large companies, banks, and financial institutions is that of Eggert Economic Enterprises. A consensus of forecasts of real GNP for the year ahead has been remarkably accurate, in large part because the sources supplying the forecasts use information from firms that generate a considerable part of the GNP. But such forecasts do not supply goals, which is what is proposed in the text.

ABOUT THE AUTHOR

ALFRED C. NEAL has spent most of his career in policy making — twenty years as president of the Committee for Economic Development (CED) working on policy problems with leaders of business, government, and academia, and ten years as an officer in the Federal Reserve. This book incorporates learning from those experiences and from frequent service on government and private, domestic and international commissions, to which there are many references in this book.

The author was educated at the University of California (Berkeley), the London School of Economics, and Brown University, where he also taught economics. He holds Ph.D. and LL.D. degrees. He has written numerous articles on economics, and is the author of and contributor to several books in that field.

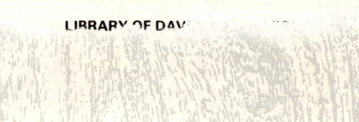